50 Walks in
OXFORDSHIRE

First published 2003
Researched and written by Nick Channer except Walks 12, 16, 17, 41
and 42, which were researched and written by Ann F Stonehouse.

Produced by AA Publishing
© Automobile Association Developments Limited 2003
Illustrations © Automobile Association Developments Limited 2003

Published by AA Publishing (a trading name of Automobile
Association Developments Limited, whose registered office is
Millstream, Maidenhead, Windsor, SL4 5GD;
registered number 1878835)

Ordnance Survey® This product includes mapping data licensed from
Ordnance Survey® with the permission of the
Controller of Her Majesty's Stationery Office.
© Crown copyright 2003. All rights reserved. Licence number 399221

ISBN 0 7495 3631 4

A01418

A CIP catalogue record for this book is available
from the British Library.

The contents of this book are believed correct at the time of printing.
Nevertheless, the publishers cannot be held responsible for any errors
or omissions or for changes in the details given in this book or for
the consequences of any reliance on the information it provides. This
does not affect your statutory rights. We have tried to ensure
accuracy in this book, but things do change and we would be grateful
if readers would advise us of any inaccuracies they may encounter.

We have taken all reasonable steps to ensure that these walks are
safe and achievable by walkers with a realistic level of fitness.
However, all outdoor activities involve a degree of risk and the
publishers accept no responsibility for any injuries caused to
readers whilst following these walks. For more advice on walking
safely see page 128. The mileage range shown on the front cover is for
guidance only – some walks may exceed or be less than these
distances.

Visit the AA Publishing website at www.theAA.com

Paste-up and editorial by Outcrop Publishing Services Ltd, Cumbria
for AA Publishing

Colour reproduction by LC Repro
Printed in Italy by G Canale & C SPA, Torino, Italy

Legend

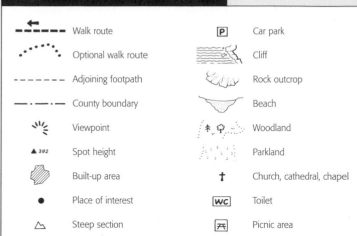

◄ - - - - -	Walk route	P	Car park
••••••	Optional walk route	≈≈≈	Cliff
- - - - - -	Adjoining footpath		Rock outcrop
— · — · —	County boundary		Beach
☀	Viewpoint		Woodland
▲ 392	Spot height		Parkland
⬤	Built-up area	†	Church, cathedral, chapel
●	Place of interest	WC	Toilet
△	Steep section	🛆	Picnic area

Oxfordshire locator map

Contents

Contents

Rating: Each walk is rated for its relative difficulty compared to the other walks in this book. Walks marked 🚶🚶🚶 are likely to be shorter and easier with little total ascent. The hardest walks are marked 🚶🚶🚶.

Walking in Safety: For advice and safety tips ➤ 128.

Introducing Oxfordshire

Located at the heart of England, Oxfordshire enjoys a rich heritage and surprisingly varied scenery. Its landscape encompasses open chalk downland and glorious beechwoods, picturesque rivers and attractive villages set in peaceful farmland.

In the south west the county meets neighbouring Berkshire high on the downs, and here there are far-reaching vistas and fascinating links with the ancient past. To the south east lie the Chilterns, their steep scarps and tree-clad hills providing a superb natural playground in this densely populated area. The countryside in the north west of Oxfordshire seems isolated by comparison, more redolent of the north of England, with its broad views, undulating landscape and dry-stone walls.

The county demonstrates how the strong influence of humans has shaped this part of England over the centuries. The Romans built villas in the pretty river valleys that thread their way through Oxfordshire, the Saxons constructed royal palaces here, and the Normans left an impressive legacy of castles and churches. The philanthropic wool merchants made their mark too, and many of their fine buildings serve as a long-lasting testimony to what they did for the good of the local community.

Like many of the English counties, Oxfordshire has witnessed its battles over the years – it was stained by the blood of the defeated Danes in the 9th century AD and ravaged by the opposing armies of the English Civil War. The struggle for power and political supremacy has produced some of history's most prominent figures. One of Oxfordshire's boldest sons, Alfred the Great, was born at Wantage, while Winston Churchill, the one man who symbolised Britain's fighting spirit during the Second World War, will always be associated with Blenheim Palace, his palatial family home and now one of Britain's greatest visitor attractions.

The majestic Thames has been described as liquid history. Rising in a Gloucestershire meadow, the fledgling river drifts towards Oxford, then heads south through Abingdon, Wallingford and Goring. In its own way Britain's most famous river has helped mould the county's distinctive character through the centuries.

Oxfordshire has two national trails – the gentle Thames Path and the timeless Ridgeway. Both routes, parts of which appear in this guide, explore the rural heart of the county, giving a unique insight into the changing face of the countryside. Elsewhere Oxfordshire is criss-crossed by a network of ancient paths and tracks,

---

PUBLIC TRANSPORT ℹ

Oxfordshire is well served by public transport, making many of the walks in this guide easily accessible. For information about bus services contact Traveline on 0870 608 2 608. Walks 5, 8, 9, 10, 17, 30, 39 and 40 start at or near a railway station. For times of trains throughout the country, call the 24-hour national train enquiry line on 08457 48 49 50. For countrywide public transport information look at the internet site www.pti.org.uk.

which evolved over the years as a vital means of communication. Different generations followed these routes to work in fields and factories, or to go to school, market and church.

Towns and cities are a feature of this book, too. The sleepy backwaters of Abingdon, Wallingford, Wantage, Watlington and Witney reveal how these old towns grew and evolved over the centuries, while Oxford's imposing streets reflect the beauty and elegance of 'that sweet city with her dreaming spires.' Fans of the famous fictional sleuth Inspector Morse will recognise many Oxford landmarks described in the books by Colin Dexter and used in the long-running television series.

Each route offers a specific theme to enhance the walk, as well as snippets of useful information on what to look for and what to do while you're there. Visitor attractions crop up on many routes; to avoid disappointment, find out opening times and if dogs are welcome before setting out. Apart from two walks, which require a train to return to the start, all are circular.

Using this Book

Information panels

An information panel for each walk shows its relative difficulty (➤ 5), the distance and total amount of ascent. An indication of the gradients you will encounter is shown by the rating ▲▲ ▲▲ ▲▲ (no steep slopes) to ▲▲ ▲▲ ▲▲ (several very steep slopes).

Maps

There are 30 maps, covering 40 of the walks. Some walks have a suggested option in the same area. The information panel for these walks will tell you how much extra walking is involved. On short-cut suggestions the panel will tell you the total distance if you set out from the start of the main walk. Where an option returns to the same point on the main walk, just the distance of the loop is given. Where an option leaves the main walk at one point and returns to it at another, then the distance shown is for the whole walk. The minimum time suggested is for reasonably fit walkers and doesn't allow for stops. Each walk has a suggested map. Laminated aqua3 maps are longer lasting and water resistant.

Start Points

The start of each walk is given as a six-figure grid reference prefixed by two letters indicating which 100km square of the National Grid it refers to. You'll find more information on grid references on most Ordnance Survey maps.

Dogs

We have tried to give dog owners useful advice about how dog friendly each walk is. Please respect other countryside users. Keep your dog under control, especially around livestock, and obey local bylaws and other dog control notices.

Car Parking

Many of the car parks suggested are public, but occasionally you may find you have to park on the roadside or in a lay-by. Please be considerate when you leave your car, ensuring that access roads or gates are not blocked and that other vehicles can pass safely. Remember that pub car parks are private and should not be used unless you have the owner's permission.

Walk 1

Broughton's Magnificent Moated Castle

Take a delightful walk across open country and through fine parkland to a splendid Tudor pile.

•DISTANCE•	2¾ miles (4.4km)
•MINIMUM TIME•	1hr 30min
•ASCENT / GRADIENT•	82ft (25m)
•LEVEL OF DIFFICULTY•	
•PATHS•	Field and parkland paths and tracks, some roads, 6 stiles
•LANDSCAPE•	Rolling farmland and parkland to south west of Banbury
•SUGGESTED MAP•	aqua3 OS Explorer 191 Banbury, Bicester & Chipping Norton
•START / FINISH•	Grid reference: SP 421384
•DOG FRIENDLINESS•	Under control across farmland and by Broughton Castle
•PARKING•	Limited spaces in Broughton village
•PUBLIC TOILETS•	Broughton Castle, for visitors; otherwise none on route

BACKGROUND TO THE WALK

One of the pleasures of walking in the countryside is that initial glimpse of a ruined church, a wonderfully eccentric folly or a distant baronial hall. The first sighting of Broughton Castle usually provokes a gasp of surprise, too, as it edges teasingly into view across an extensive swathe of green lawns and classic English parkland.

The castle was originally built as a fortified manor house by Sir John de Broughton early in the 14th century. Later it passed to William de Wykeham, the famous founding father of Winchester College and New College, Oxford, who set about converting the manor house into a castle, designing battlements and a gatehouse among other additions. One of Broughton's greatest attributes is its 14th-century private chapel, approached by a stone staircase from the groined passage.

In the 15th century, Broughton passed by marriage to the Fiennes (pronounced 'Fines') family when the granddaughter of Sir Thomas Wykeham, great-nephew and heir of William, married William Fiennes, 2nd Lord Saye and Sele. During the Elizabethan era the house was transformed virtually beyond recognition into the Tudor building you see today.

Subtle Support

During the Civil War, the Fiennes family were staunch supporters of the Parliamentarians and did much to defend this corner of Oxfordshire. The 1st Viscount Saye and Sele, demonstrating caution and common sense, was dubbed 'Old Subtlety', and it was within the walls of the castle, in the Council Chamber, that Puritan leaders such as Pym, Hampden, Vane and Essex met to plot the Great Rebellion and thwart Charles I. Saye and Sele raised his own regiment of dragoons, known as Lord Saye's Bluecoats after the colour of their uniform, from among his tenantry. Together with his four sons, he fought at the Battle of Edgehill in 1642, but soon afterwards the castle was besieged and captured. The distinctive compound title of Saye and Sele dates from the original creation of the barony in 1447.

Members of the Fiennes dynasty still live at Broughton Castle, which is open to the public (not daily – check for opening times), and today the name takes on even greater significance. Ralph and Joseph, both well-known and well-respected film and stage actors, are members of the family.

Not surprisingly, the castle often crops up as an imposing backdrop in film and television productions. Perhaps most notable on the list of credits is the 1998 film *Shakespeare in Love* in which Broughton Castle appears as Viola's stately home. The dance, where Will first meets her, was filmed in the Great Hall, with its beautiful plaster ceiling and hanging bosses, while it is in the Oak Room that Wessex tells Viola that she is to be married. For outdoor scenes, an artificial balcony, overlooking formal gardens, was constructed, representing part of Viola's bedroom.

Walk 1

Walk 1 Directions

① Keep **Wykeham Lane** on your right and parkland on the left and walk through the village of **Broughton**. Pass **Danvers Road** on the right-hand side, followed by **Danvers Cottage** on the left and, when the road curves right just beyond the cottage, swing left over a stile, signposted 'North Newington'.

Keep ahead across the field to reach a stile in the next boundary, then carry straight on in the next field to cross a footbridge in the trees. This is sometimes obscured by foliage during the summer months. Continue ahead, keeping a line of trees on your right-hand side and, three-quarters of the way along the field boundary, look for a footbridge on the right.

WHERE TO EAT AND DRINK ⓘ

The **Saye and Sele Arms** in Broughton, refurbished in 2002, is a popular, characterful pub offering everything from sandwiches to steaks. As well as the dining area, there is a garden where you can relax over a drink after the walk. Food is not available on Sunday evening. The **Blinking Owl** at North Newington is cosy on a cold winter's day, and has traditional ales and a good menu. There is a tea room at **Broughton Castle**.

---

② Cross the footbridge, followed by a concrete track, to reach another stile, and head diagonally right across the field to a minor road. Take the right of way on the opposite side and follow a stretch of the **Macmillan Way** between fields to reach a stile. Cross the stile to the lane and turn left. Walk towards the village of **North Newington**, passing the entrance to **Park Farm** on your right-hand side. Pass the **Blinking Owl** pub and **Wheelwright Cottage** and then turn left into **The Pound**, opposite the old village pump.

③ Walk past **Pound Cottage** and look for a footpath which starts about 30yds (27m) beyond it on the right-hand side. Follow the footpath diagonally right across the field to reach a wide, obvious gap in the hedgerow on the far side. Turn left to reach another gap in the

---

WHILE YOU'RE THERE ⓘ

Visit **Banbury**, the second largest town in Oxfordshire, renowned for its historic buildings and different architectural styles. Banbury's new museum occupies an attractive canalside setting and its modern displays illustrate the town's origins and colourful past. The Civil War and Banbury's manufacturing industry are covered.

---

hedge, then head obliquely right in the field, making for the top corner, which is defined by trees and hedgerow. Pass through the gate and keep ahead, with the field boundary on your immediate left. Walk along to the next gate and then down the field to the road.

④ Cross over the road to a galvanised gate and follow the track towards some barns. Keep to the left of these buildings and look for a stile and footpath branching off to the left, running hard by a fence on the right-hand side. Follow the path to reach a stile in the far boundary and cross over into the parkland of **Broughton Castle**. Soon the spire of Broughton church and the outline of the castle and its moat come into sight ahead of you. Continue ahead across the parkland and down to meet the castle drive. Head for a gate into the churchyard and then follow a path to reach the **B4035** on the outskirts of Broughton. Turn left along the road and return to the start of the walk in the village centre.

WHAT TO LOOK FOR ⓘ

As you cross the parkland towards Broughton Castle, look for the spire of Broughton's **Church of St Mary**, its imposing tower crowned by a fine spire. The church dates mainly from the 14th century and includes an elaborate painted tomb of Sir John de Broughton.

From Cottisford to Juniper Hill with Flora Thompson

Visit two villages vividly brought to life through the books of a remarkable local writer.

•DISTANCE•	4¾ miles (7.7km)
•MINIMUM TIME•	2hrs
•ASCENT / GRADIENT•	90ft (27m)
•LEVEL OF DIFFICULTY•	
•PATHS•	Tracks, field paths, stretches of quiet country roads, 2 stiles
•LANDSCAPE•	Quiet farmland to south of Brackley
•SUGGESTED MAP•	aqua3 OS Explorer 191 Banbury, Bicester & Chipping Norton
•START / FINISH•	Grid reference: SP 591312
•DOG FRIENDLINESS•	On lead in Cottisford and Juniper Hill and near pheasants
•PARKING•	Restricted parking in Cottisford
•PUBLIC TOILETS•	None on route

BACKGROUND TO THE WALK

Flora June Timms was one of thousands of children growing up in rural north east Oxfordshire in the latter part of the 19th century. But Flora was blessed with a rare gift. She had an observant eye and a sharp awareness of her surroundings. As a girl, she studied the daily routine closely – the minutiae of everyday life in a traditional English village.

Magical Memories

Years later, as Flora Thompson, a married woman in her sixties, she began writing sketches of her precious childhood which later became the basis for three famous books – *Lark Rise* (Juniper Hill), *Over to Candleford* (an amalgam of nearby Banbury, Bicester and Buckingham) and *Candleford Green*. The stories were published during the Second World War and then in 1945 as a trilogy – *Lark Rise to Candleford*. Even today her work is seen as a brilliantly crafted social record of the times, expertly capturing the spirit and essence of rural life during the closing stages of the Victorian era.

A Country Childhood

Flora was born at Juniper Hill in 1876, the eldest of ten children. Her father was a stonemason who worked in Brackley and her mother had once been employed locally as a nursemaid. From the age of seven, Flora attended the local school at neighbouring Cottisford. She walked there and back from Juniper Hill with other children from the village. 'Up the long, straight road they straggled, in twos and threes and in gangs, their flat, rush dinner-baskets over their shoulders and their shabby coats on their arms against the rain.' The village school is now a private house.

Every Sunday Flora attended church at Cottisford with her brother Edwin, sitting in their grandfather's pew opposite the door. At the age of 14, she left school and went to work as a post office assistant at nearby Fringford. It proved to be a good move for young Flora.

She made use of her employer's library, developing and expanding her knowledge and understanding of literature. Mrs Whitton 'had more influence than anyone in shaping the outward course of my life', she wrote.

Flora's Rise to Fame

At the age of 20, Flora left Juniper Hill to work at a post office in Surrey. She later moved to Essex and then to Hampshire, where she met and married John Thompson, a junior post office clerk. They had three children, Winifred, Basil and Peter. In 1928 John became postmaster in Dartmouth.

Now firmly established in the West Country, Flora began writing, recalling the days of her childhood in Juniper Hill. But tragedy was to overwhelm Flora. During the Second World War, her younger son, Peter, joined the Merchant Navy and was killed when his ship was torpedoed. Flora never fully recovered from the shock.

A Fitting Tribute

After the war, having written *Still Glides the Stream* – her final work – Flora developed pneumonia, which left her with a weak heart. She died in 1947, aged 70. A festival was held at Cottisford in 1976 to mark her centenary and two years later a stage version of *Lark Rise* was performed by the National Theatre.

Walk 2 Directions

① Keep the postbox and telephone box on the right and follow the road through **Cottisford**. Pass the church on your right and, when the road swings round to the right, branch left at the entrance to **College Farm**. Keep the farm outbuildings on your left and follow the track, which runs between tall hedges. Continue to a gap in the hedgerow on the right and turn right to join a bridleway.

WHILE YOU'RE THERE ⓘ

As you reach the buildings of Juniper Hill, turn right along the drive to a cottage called Queenies. Look to the side of it and you'll see the **cottage** where Flora Thompson lived as a child. Then retrace your steps and continue along to the road opposite Larkwell.

② Keep trees, a ditch and a hedgerow on your right-hand side and, further on, the bridleway cuts between margins of bracken. Pass alongside a plantation to reach a junction with a track. Ahead of you are the buildings of **Tusmore Park**. Turn right and walk along to a left bend. Swing right here to join a waymarked footpath, then bear left almost immediately. Keep alongside a wire fence and, on reaching the corner, go straight ahead over a footbridge.

③ Head north, keeping trees and hedgerow on the right, and eventually you come to a track. Go straight on to reach some double wooden gates and a stile. Cross the road beyond and take the path on the opposite side signposted to Juniper Hill. Follow the right of way leading across the fields. Over to the left, in the

distance, are the dishes of Croughton Wireless Station. Approaching **Juniper Hill**, join a drive serving some bungalows. Keep ahead to the road and turn right opposite a cottage called **Larkwell** (if you wish, you can pay a visit to Flora Thompson's Cottage at this point, ► While You're There).

WHAT TO LOOK FOR ⓘ

Stop off at **St Mary's Church** in Cottisford and see the brass war memorial which faces you as you enter the building. The name at the bottom is that of Edwin Timms, who was Flora's younger brother, killed in action at the Battle of the Somme in 1916. Flora called St Mary's a 'little squat church'.

④ Pass the former village inn, the Fox, and continue along the road as far as the village sign for **Juniper Hill**. Turn right just beyond it at the sign for Cottisford. Follow the path which runs between allotments, then cross a stile and head diagonally left across a large field, making for a curtain of woodland in the distance. Look for a track in the corner and cut between trees to the next field. Keep right, alongside the edge of the woodland, with a ditch just beside you. Cross into the next field and continue all the way to meet the road. Turn left opposite the **Manor House** and return to the centre of **Cottisford** and the start of the walk.

WHERE TO EAT AND DRINK ⓘ

There are no pubs on the actual route. Try the **Butchers Arms** at nearby Fringford, a cosy pub selling books about the village and Flora Thompson's connection with it. The Butchers Arms offers a good range of meals and snacks, including a choice of substantial sandwiches, with smoked salmon and cream cheese among the fillings.

Bewitched Otmoor – the Forgotten Land

Explore a desolate landscape, perhaps more reminiscent of the East Anglian fens than Oxfordshire.

•DISTANCE•	4 miles (6.4km)
•MINIMUM TIME•	1hr 30min
•ASCENT / GRADIENT•	Negligible
•LEVEL OF DIFFICULTY•	
•PATHS•	Country road, tracks and paths
•LANDSCAPE•	Remote wetland and farmland
•SUGGESTED MAP•	aqua3 OS Explorer 180 Oxford
•START / FINISH•	Grid reference: SP 563157
•DOG FRIENDLINESS•	Under control in vicinity of firing range. On lead on alternative linking paths across Otmoor
•PARKING•	Spaces near church at Charlton-on-Otmoor
•PUBLIC TOILETS•	None on route

BACKGROUND TO THE WALK

A stone's throw to the north of Oxford lies Otmoor, a canvas of fields and hedgerows that seems to have been bypassed by the rest of the county. A curious ghostly stillness pervades this wilderness, inspiring various writers over the years to describe it romantically as 'the forgotten land', 'bewitched Otmoor' and 'sleeping Otmoor cast under a spell of ancient magic.'

An Abandoned Landscape

Some of it is sheltered and here you can savour the rural charm of green lanes and quiet woodland. Now and again there are signs of life too – the rifle range and the seven villages scattered on various elevations overlooking the perimeter of the moor. The residents once used Otmoor's unpromising terrain for grazing cattle and for wildfowling, fishing and collecting fuel. But mostly it is an austere, abandoned landscape over which the passage of time has had little influence.

With its flat fields, ditches and dykes, it is, in places, reminiscent of East Anglia. On a cold winter's day, and even occasionally in high summer, you can sense Otmoor's sinister, sometimes unsettling, atmosphere. At times it is dark and mysterious, at times it exudes an air of calm and tranquillity. Cross Otmoor as a light mist drifts over the meadows and you'll find the image will linger long in the memory.

Alice's Giant Chessboard

If time allows, journey to the village of Beckley, perched 400ft (122m) over the southern edge of Otmoor, and you'll see why Lewis Carroll was supposedly inspired by the view of this primitive 4,000-acre (1,620ha) landscape to write about the giant chessboard in *Alice Through the Looking Glass*. John Buchan, who lived at nearby Elsfield, described Otmoor in great detail in his novel *The Blanket of the Dark*.

Otmoor for Ever

Centuries ago, Otmoor was waterlogged during much of the year. However, by the late 1820s the moor had been drained and enclosed for agricultural use, as a result of the efforts of landowners. But this was met with fierce opposition from the local commoners, leading to serious rioting in the area. The rioters, who for so long had been allowed to graze livestock on the common land of Otmoor, moved in and destroyed new fences, hedges, gates and bridges. But it was a pointless exercise.

Police and troops were drafted in to help tackle the problem and eventually the rioters acknowledged defeat and withdrew. Nearly 50 local villagers were arrested and taken to Oxford, which happened to be staging its annual St Giles' Fair. The crowds sided with the rioters, shouting 'Otmoor for ever'.

Paradise Reprieved

In the 1980s the moor was at the centre of a bitter row once again, when it was under threat from a proposal to build a new motorway extension. After much opposition, the threat was lifted in order to accommodate a rare butterfly whose breeding ground is Otmoor. In fact the whole area is a paradise for birdwatchers and botanists, and there are many species of birds and plants here. Besides the various resident bird species, many more pass through on a fly-line from the Severn to the Wash.

Walk 3 Directions

① Keep the church on the right and walk through the village of **Charlton-on-Otmoor**. Pass **Blacksmiths Lane** and **College Court** and continue on the road. Follow the lane between hedgerows and fields. Soon you reach the sign for Oddington. When the road bends right, branch off to the left by a telephone box, following the sign for Horton-cum-Studley.

WHAT TO LOOK FOR ⓘ

There is a **military firing range** on Otmoor. Look for written information about the range at the side of the path and follow the advice carefully. The Emperor moth, marsh fritillary butterflies and Black Hairstreak are among a number of **rare insects** found on Otmoor. Take a walk across the moor and you may find the landscape partially puckered with **holes** from the Second World War bombing practice – a far cry from the serenity of today.

---

② Take the track out of the village, crossing a concrete bridge after a short walk. At the next junction, just beyond it, avoid the galvanised gates on the right, and follow the parallel bridleway, cutting between ditches and hedges. Pass a stile on the left, leading to a linking path which provides an alternative route to the wetlands of Otmoor. The tower of Charlton-on-Otmoor church can be seen at intervals along the track. Continue to the signs for Otmoor's military **firing range**. Keep ahead until you reach a gate on the left and several gates on the right.

③ Turn left at this point and follow the old Roman road north. The track is broad and can be wet in winter. When it curves right, branch off to the left and begin the last leg of the walk.

WHILE YOU'RE THERE ⓘ

St Mary's Church at Charlton-on-Otmoor is a fine medieval building with a tall tower which is a useful landmark when walking on Otmoor. The building is Grade I listed and mentioned in the book *England's 1000 Best Churches* by Simon Jenkins.

---

④ Follow the path through the trees and soon it broadens to a track cutting between fields and hedgerows. There are good views across a broad expanse of Otmoor to the south. Cross a wooden footbridge and continue on the track. Turn right by some corrugated barns and make for Charlton-on-Otmoor. The church tower is clearly visible now. Cross the **New River Ray** and climb the slope to the junction. Turn left by the **Crown** and return to the church in the centre of the village.

WHERE TO EAT AND DRINK ⓘ

The **Crown** in Charlton-on-Otmoor serves meals and traditional bar food. The only pub on the walk, the Crown benefits from a popular beer garden. Many of the pubs in the nearby villages serve food, including the **Nut Tree Inn** at Murcott, the **Abingdon Arms** at Beckley and the **Red Lion** at Islip.

Noke – at the Oak Trees

Make for a sleepy village hidden along the edge of Otmoor.
See map and information panel for Walk 3

•DISTANCE•	8 miles (12.9km)
•MINIMUM TIME•	3hrs
•ASCENT / GRADIENT•	Negligible
•LEVEL OF DIFFICULTY•	

Walk 4 Directions (Walk 3 option)

Keep ahead on the road through Oddington, following it as it bends sharp right by a telephone box, then round to the left (Point Ⓐ). On the left is **Oddington church**, whose past rectors include Gilbert Sheldon (1598–1677). Sheldon was appointed Bishop of London in 1660 and Archbishop of Canterbury three years later. He became Chancellor at Oxford and also donated £12,200 to build the city's Sheldonian Theatre.

Pass the church and continue along the lane. Look for a path, hidden by foliage in summer, beyond the next bend in the road, and go through a dilapidated kissing gate. After several paces, the path reaches the corner of a field. Cut diagonally right across it towards the far corner, making for the end of a line of trees. Keep to the right of **Logg Farm**, join a drive for a few paces, then swing right at the waymark, following a track. As it curves left towards a detached house, go straight on across the field, passing under power lines. Keep the fence on your left. Cross a track to a waymark and keep to the left field boundary, looking for a footbridge in the corner.

Cross the **River Ray** (Point Ⓑ) to a second footbridge and turn right to skirt the field edge. Keep the water on your right and approach a gap in the field boundary. Keep this side of it, turn left and head south, keeping the hedge on your immediate right. Join a track by a circular tank and keep ahead. Follow the right of way between hedgerows, and veer left at a fork. Where the track curves right towards **Manor Farm**, go straight on along a grassy path left of the outbuildings. Head for a junction with the **Oxfordshire Way** and go straight on to the road (Point Ⓒ).

Keep left, pass **Rectory Cottage** and walk through **Noke** (meaning 'at the oak trees'), avoiding a path to Woodeaton. The font at St Giles Church was given by the lady of the manor, Gundreda, a daughter of William the Conqueror.

Continue on the lane, passing a sign for **Lower Farm**. Follow the drive towards the farm buildings, branching left before them at the fork. Go straight on when you reach a bend. At the next junction, turn left and follow the grassy track, which later narrows to a path. Keep ahead when you reach a clear track and follow it to the next junction by galvanised gates. Turn right and rejoin Walk 3 at Point ②.

Rousham's Classic Garden

A walk that includes a delightful garden and a stretch of inland waterway.

•DISTANCE•	5 miles (8km)
•MINIMUM TIME•	1hr 45min
•ASCENT / GRADIENT•	150ft (46m) ▲ ▲ ▲
•LEVEL OF DIFFICULTY•	🚶 🚶 🚶
•PATHS•	Field paths, tow path and road (can be busy), 5 stiles
•LANDSCAPE•	Pretty countryside with Oxford Canal and River Cherwell
•SUGGESTED MAP•	aqua3 OS Explorer 191 Banbury, Bicester & Chipping Norton
•START / FINISH•	Grid reference: SP 476260
•DOG FRIENDLINESS•	On lead near livestock, under control on tow path
•PARKING•	Recreation ground car park at Steeple Aston
•PUBLIC TOILETS•	Rousham House, for visitors; otherwise none on route

Walk 5 Directions

From the car park, turn left and walk down the street (**Paines Hill**) through the village of Steeple Aston to the T-junction. The post office and shop are on the corner and across the way is the White Lion pub. Turn right into **South Side** and pass **Jubilee Close**. Carry on ahead until you see a footpath on the left signposted for Rousham. Join a tarmac drive here and follow it as it dwindles to a track that heads south. When it runs into a field, continue ahead on a waymarked path cutting across pastures. Make for a gap in the hedgerow and follow the path through the undergrowth, across two stiles and down into the next field.

Keep woodland over to the left and aim for the far left corner of the field and a stile leading out to the road. Cross over and go up the bank, turning left at the top. Follow the path through the trees to a stile leading into a large field. Cross it diagonally, making for a gate by a farm. Exit to the road and turn right to visit **Rousham House** or left to continue the walk.

The lovely Cherwell Valley is the perfect setting for this splendid mansion. Built by Sir Robert Dormer in 1635, on an H-plan, the house was remodelled by William Kent just over 100 years later with an air of free Gothic style about it. Kent was a coach-painter's apprentice who became an architect and landscape gardener. He designed Horse Guards, the famous London landmark, in 1745.

The garden at Rousham is a lasting monument to the work of Kent and a fine example of English landscape design. Here, the River Cherwell flows through 30 acres (12ha) of garden, which has more than a hint of the Italianate. Among the many features are cascades and ponds, groves, the Temple of Echo and the seven-arched portico known as Praeneste. No wonder Horace Walpole called it 'Kentissimo'.

A peaceful stroll along Long Walk is one of Rousham's most popular attractions, and inside the house there are many treasures too, including a panelled oak chamber and a painted parlour, originally a small 17th-century kitchen.

As you leave Rousham, walk along to the church located in a peaceful setting a short distance from the main house. Enter the churchyard and at once there is a poignant reminder of the sheer futility of the First World War. On the right are the graves of two young men killed in battle, members of the Cottrell-Dormer family of Rousham House.

WHERE TO EAT AND DRINK ⓘ

Picnicking is permitted within the gardens of **Rousham House**. If you prefer pubs, try the **White Lion** at Steeple Aston, or the **Bell** at Lower Heyford, which dates back to 1602 and was once a chapel. There is the usual choice of ales, snacks and more substantial fare.

Follow the road down to the traffic-lights and turn right just beyond them. Cross the **River Cherwell** and look to your right for a splendid view of Rousham House framed by trees. Pass the entrance to Heyford railway station and follow the road over the railway and the parallel Oxford Canal. Turn left immediately beyond it, by **Canal Cottage**, and follow the path back over the canal to join the tow path. Look for the tower of Lower Heyford church and keep ahead to a swing bridge, which allows access to the village.

Continue on the tow path, pass **Allen's Lock** and make for **bridge No 203**. Turn left for a few paces, then veer right in the field to a bridge over the river. Keep the water on your right and look for a railway embankment ahead. Pass under the railway bridge and cross the field to a footbridge and stile set against a curtain of trees.

Go up the bank and the field slope towards trees in the top boundary. Cut through them into the next field, keeping right here. The **Rousham Eyecatcher** is a useful directional landmark at this point. Alone and forgotten in the middle of a field, again the work of William Kent, its sudden appearance on the brow of the hill catches you by surprise, leaving you wondering what it is meant to signify.

The Eyecatcher is a buttressed three-arched ruin or sham, instantly reminiscent of a castle gateway and visible on the skyline – hence the name. Like follies, they were once fashionable with whimsical landowners and colourful eccentrics. The Rousham Eyecatcher's solitary position makes it hard to find for anyone other than those passing this way on foot. Nevertheless, it consolidates Kent's undisputed creative genius.

Follow the boundary down and round to a gate. Join a track and turn right. Head up to the edge of **Steeple Aston**, turn right at the junction and return to the car park.

WHILE YOU'RE THERE ⓘ

Make a brief detour to the charming village of **Lower Heyford**, formerly Heyford Purcell, after the Purcell family who moved here from nearby Newton Purcell. The village was once an important river crossing on the Cherwell, especially at hay harvest time – the name is probably derived from 'hay ford'. The stone bridge replaced the ford and was constructed during the 13th century.

Hook Norton's Towering Success

Explore delightful ironstone country before visiting one of Oxfordshire's more unusual buildings.

•DISTANCE•	4½ miles (7.2km)
•MINIMUM TIME•	2hrs
•ASCENT / GRADIENT•	164ft (50m) ▲ ▲ ▲
•LEVEL OF DIFFICULTY•	🚶 🚶 🚶
•PATHS•	Field paths, tracks and bridleways, quiet roads
•LANDSCAPE•	Undulating countryside close to Warwickshire border
•SUGGESTED MAP•	aqua3 OS Explorer 191 Banbury, Bicester & Chipping Norton
•START / FINISH•	Grid reference: SP 355330
•DOG FRIENDLINESS•	Under control on farmland and on lead where requested
•PARKING•	Spaces in Hook Norton village centre
•PUBLIC TOILETS•	Hook Norton Brewery Visitor Centre

BACKGROUND TO THE WALK

Hook Norton is one of those places that you are most likely to stumble upon by accident. Hidden away down winding lanes a few miles from the Cotswold town of Chipping Norton, this sizeable village, one of the largest parishes in Oxfordshire, is typical of many other settlements in the county – with one possible exception.

Tucked away in Brewery Lane, on the edge of the village, is the Hook Norton Brewery, displaying one of the most distinctive and unusual Victorian façades in the country. The tower brewing building, erected at the turn of the last century, has been described as 'an essay in brick, ironstone, slate, weather-boarding, half timber and cast iron.'

Following Tradition

During the 19th century it was traditional for most towns, cities and even large villages to have their own brewery. During the 1880s Oxfordshire alone had almost 50. Today, the scarcity of independent breweries reflects the changing fortunes of the licensed trade. However, the Hook Norton Brewery has managed to fight off the big corporate companies and remain successful.

It was during the Victorian era, in 1849, that John Harris set up in business as a maltster by brewing beer in a nearby farmhouse. A year later, Harris built his own brewhouse, where he used pure Cotswold spring water. He soon found there was a great demand for his beer and so he established a small brewery with its own maltings.

Growing the Business

When Harris died, his son and nephew assumed responsibility for the running of the business and by 1899 work on the present tower brewery was complete. The new building, comprising six floors, housed the latest brewing equipment and allowed the entire brewing sequence to be undertaken as a continuous process. It was at this time that John Harris and

Company became the Hook Norton Brewery Company Limited. Following the death of John Harris, the task of running the brewery fell to his son-in-law Alban Clarke, who was killed in a motorcycle accident in 1917. Hook Norton remains a family business in the 21st century. The brewery is now run by Clarke's grandson, David, while his son, James, is Head Brewer and a director of the company.

There is nothing brash or hi-tech about Hook Norton. Much of the brewery's intricate machinery is original – the process of brewing has been the same for over 100 years and apart from a new laboratory, stainless-steel copper and cooling system, little has changed. One of the brewery's greatest assets is the mighty steam-driven, 25-horse-power piston engine, dating back to 1899. Today the Hook Norton Brewery has 42 tied houses and 42 employees. In September 1999, 100 years after brewing began in the existing building, Princess Anne opened a new visitor centre and museum, housed in the original maltings.

Walk 6 Directions

① With the church on your left, turn right into **Middle Hill**. Follow it down to the next road and keep

ahead to the bridge. Turn left into **Park Road** and follow it to the next junction. Continue ahead, keeping a row of bungalows on the left. When the road bends sharp left, join a waymarked bridleway and follow it out of Hook Norton. Pass the remains of the old railway viaduct and walk along to **Park Farm**.

② Cross a cattle grid and continue for about 50yds (46m). When the track forks, keep left and follow the path to a gate. Continue along the field edge to the next gate and follow the obvious track as it curves to the right. Cross a ford at the footbridge and make for the next gate. Follow the field boundary and cross into the next field, keeping trees and a hedgerow on the left. Head for a galvanised gate and swing right at the bridleway sign. Head diagonally across the field and look for a gate in the trees in the top boundary. Follow the grassy path alongside the fence to reach a drive.

WHERE TO EAT AND DRINK

There are several pubs to choose from in Hook Norton. The **Sun Inn** and the **Bell** both serve food and are both situated in the village centre. On the outskirts of Hook Norton, close to the brewery, lies the **Pear Tree Inn**, a brewery house since 1869. Low ceilings, beams and horse brasses add to the charm and character of the bar and outside is a popular beer garden. Light refreshments are served at the **Hook Norton Brewery Visitor Centre**.

---

③ Turn right here, away from **Cradle Farm**, and walk along to some outbuildings at the point where the drive bends sharp left. Keep right here and follow the track

alongside a pair of semi-detached houses on the right. Emerge from the trees to three tracks; take the middle track up the slope between fences to reach the road. Cross over to a galvanised gate and follow the bridleway between fences, trees and paddocks. On reaching a gate turn right to a wrought-iron gate leading into a field. Turn left and make for a further gate into the next field. Pass to the right-hand side of some fencing and make for a gate in the field boundary.

④ Turn right to join an avenue of lime trees. At length the drive reaches the road. Turn left, then take the first right for Hook Norton. At the first junction, turn right at the sign for Swerford and walk along to **Hook Norton Cutting**. Retrace your steps to the junction and continue ahead towards **Hook Norton**. Pass the speed restriction sign and keep ahead into the village. Pass **Park Road** on the right and take **Middle Hill** back up to the church and the pubs.

WHAT TO LOOK FOR

As you leave Hook Norton, near the start of the walk, keep an eye out for the remains of an old **railway viaduct** on the disused Banbury-to-Cheltenham line. Seven stone pillars serve as a sad reminder of the golden age of rail travel. A key factor in the success of the brewery during its early years was the welcome presence of navvies who were engaged in the building of the line between 1865 and 1888.

WHILE YOU'RE THERE

Tours of the **Hook Norton Brewery** are by prior arrangement and take place in the morning. Take a stroll along to the **Hook Norton Cutting**, now a nature reserve. The site is managed by the local wildlife trust, the only voluntary organisation in the region concerned with all aspects of local wildlife conservation. The wildlife trust manages more than 90 reserves within the Oxfordshire, Berkshire and Buckinghamshire region, which are the haunt of rare and endangered species.

The Village of Great Tew – a Rare Plot

Take a stroll through one of Oxfordshire's loveliest villages before exploring undulating countryside to the south.

•DISTANCE•	4 miles (6.4km)
•MINIMUM TIME•	1hr 45min
•ASCENT / GRADIENT•	150ft (46m)
•LEVEL OF DIFFICULTY•	
•PATHS•	Field paths and tracks, stretches of quiet road, 3 stiles
•LANDSCAPE•	Rolling parkland and farmland on edge of Cotswolds
•SUGGESTED MAP•	aqua3 OS Explorer 191 Banbury, Bicester & Chipping Norton
•START / FINISH•	Grid reference: SP 395293
•DOG FRIENDLINESS•	Under control across farmland
•PARKING•	Free car park in Great Tew
•PUBLIC TOILETS•	None on route

BACKGROUND TO THE WALK

Arthur Mee, in his book *The King's England – Oxfordshire*, says that 'if our England is a garden, Great Tew is one of its rare plots.' Most would agree. The village is one of the most beautiful in Oxfordshire, a gem of a place that has to be seen to be fully appreciated.

The Fall and Rise of Great Tew

Originally designed as an estate village in the 19th century, with the intention of blending architectural beauty with utility and agricultural management, Great Tew went into decline in later years and virtually became derelict. However, the village has been given a new lease of life, with many of the thatched and ironstone cottages painstakingly restored, and now Great Tew is a designated Conservation Area.

The origin of its name is unclear, but Tew is thought to mean 'ridge', of which there are a great many in the area. The village has a fascinating history. In 1036, 53 tenants lived here. By 1276 it had expanded to become a community of at least 75 households. However, the population fell during the 14th century, possibly as a result of the plague.

Falkland's Manor

In later years the village became closely associated with Lucius Carey, 2nd Viscount Falkland. In the 17th century the manor of Great Tew was inherited by the Viscount, a renowned classical scholar, poet and generous host who moved in elite circles. Falkland later became Secretary of State to Charles I but was killed in 1643 aged 33, serving as an ordinary trooper in the first Battle of Newbury. A later owner, G F Stratton, who inherited Great Tew in 1800, resided in a rather modest late 17th- or early 18th-century house which stood at the southern end of the village. During the early years of the 19th century, Stratton engaged in an ill-fated experiment in estate management, drawing his inspiration from the Scottish agricultural theoriest J C Loudon.

The estate subsequently changed hands several times before being acquired by Matthew Robinson Boulton, son of James Watt's partner and one of the giants of the Industrial Revolution, who had a keen eye on its sporting potential. Outlying farms were extensively rebuilt, cottages in the village were re-thatched and other features such as mullioned windows and stone door heads were added. The estate remained the home of the Boulton family for many years. Between 1914 and 1962 Great Tew was administered by trustees on behalf of two unmarried Boulton sisters, but by now the local workforce had decreased and the estate was all but abandoned.

Robb to the Rescue

It was Major Eustace Robb, an old Etonian and descendant of the Boulton family, who moved to the village with the aim of halting its steady decline. His efforts certainly paid off. A stroll through the village today is marked by a conspicuous air of affluence, with coach parties of tourists breaking their journey here to admire one of Oxfordshire's loveliest village attractions.

The noted political editor John Sergeant spent his childhood at Great Tew. His father was the rector of St Michael's Church during the middle years of the 20th century and Sergeant remembers his time here with great affection. In his memoirs, he describes Great Tew as the ideal place in which to grow up.

Walk 7 Directions

① From the car park turn left, pass the turning to Great Tew, follow the road as it bends right and as it straightens out turn right at the footpath sign, signposted 'Little Tew'. Go diagonally across the field, heading for farm outbuildings on the brow of the hill. Cross a stile in front of them to a gate and stile and keep the field boundary on the right. Follow it along to a pair of galvanised gates and a stile leading out to the road at a junction.

WHILE YOU'RE THERE ⓘ

Walk along the splendid avenue of laurels and traveller's joy leading to Great Tew's fine **medieval church**, which lies peacefully amid the trees of the parkland. The church walk was originally the carriage drive to the mansion of Lucius Carey, 2nd Viscount Falkland.

---

② Cross over and take the path, again signposted to Little Tew. Head diagonally across the field, passing to the right of a **transmitter**. On reaching the road, turn right and walk down the hill into **Little Tew**. Pass through the village and turn left at the turning for Enstone. On the corner is the **Church of St John the Evangelist**.

③ Follow the road out of Little Tew and look for the entrance to **The Lodge** on the left. Continue for a few paces to some white railings, then turn immediately left at an opening in the hedge leading into a field. Keep along the left boundary and make for a galvanised gate in the field corner. Continue ahead on the grassy path, passing a house over on the left. Keep ahead on the clear track to a kissing gate leading out to the road.

④ Cross over and follow the track signposted to Sandford. Keep alongside trees and then round to the left towards a house. As you approach it, turn right and join another track heading south east. Keep the fence on the right and make for a gate by some trees. Continue for a few paces to a gate and waymark on the left. Take the path, keeping a belt of woodland and the field edge on your left. Beyond the trees, continue ahead into the next field, again beside a tongue of woodland. Pass into the next field and continue alongside trees. Approach a **lodge** and keep to the left of it.

WHERE TO EAT AND DRINK ⓘ

With its flagstone floor, high-backed settles and inglenook fireplace, the 500-year-old **Falkland Arms** at Great Tew is one of the county's finest inns. Expect a straightforward lunchtime menu and a variety of home-made specials. Book for dinner in the evening.

---

⑤ Follow the drive to meet the road, cross over to the junction and take the turning signposted for Great Tew. Pass the entrance to **St Michael's Church**, which lies peacefully amid the trees of the parkland on the right (▶ While You're There). Look for the **village school**, also on the right, and then, just beyond the turning to Great Tew, return to the car park at the start of the walk.

WHAT TO LOOK FOR ⓘ

Little Tew is worth close inspection. The church, built by George Street, dates back to 1835 and the Methodist chapel to 1871. The Grange, also by Street, was built as a vicarage about the same time as the church. The school and almshouses were constructed in the 1860s.

Walk 8

Oxford – Heavenly Jerusalem

Explore the quiet corners and hidden backwaters of this beautiful city.

•DISTANCE•	2¼ miles (3.6km)
•MINIMUM TIME•	1hr 15min
•ASCENT / GRADIENT•	Negligible
•LEVEL OF DIFFICULTY•	
•PATHS•	Pavements, field and riverside paths, 2 stiles
•LANDSCAPE•	Urban, field and meadow on city outskirts
•SUGGESTED MAP•	aqua3 OS Explorer 180 Oxford
•START / FINISH•	Grid reference: SP 513062
•DOG FRIENDLINESS•	Not much fun in Oxford; under control elsewhere
•PARKING•	Parking in city centre, or use park-and-ride, or travel by train
•PUBLIC TOILETS•	Various in Oxford, including Westgate Shopping Centre

BACKGROUND TO THE WALK

Likened by Thomas Hardy's Jude to 'the heavenly Jerusalem', Oxford's history, beauty and tradition are admired throughout the world, ranking in importance alongside Rome, Athens and Paris. Even when its scholars have moved on to make their mark elsewhere, they return time after time to embrace and savour that curiously indefinable 'spirit of Oxford'.

From the top of its highest buildings you begin to realise that Oxford, like Florence, lies at the bottom of a shallow bowl encircled by gentle, protective hills. Originally known as Oxnaforda, Oxford was a settlement of some importance long before the university came into being. It began with the foundation of St Frideswide's nunnery in the 8th century AD and was first mentioned by name in the Anglo-Saxon Chronicle of 912, which records that King Edward the Elder had made it a fortified frontier position in his defence of Wessex when it was feared that the Danes might attack from the north.

The settlement grew and, after the Norman Conquest of 1066, King William appointed his comrade in arms, Robert d'Oilly, to be Oxford's governor. However, it was at the end of the 12th century, when Henry II prevented English clerks from attending the University of Paris, that scholars looked upon Oxford, by then one of the nine most important towns in the country, as somewhere suitable to continue their studies.

Oxford University does not exist as such. Each college is virtually autonomous, with its own rules and administration. It is the treasured and world-famous landmarks that form the real core of the university – in the compact heart of the city you'll find a hugely varied assortment of ancient buildings and monuments, among them the Radcliffe Camera, the Sheldonian Theatre, the Divinity School and the Bodleian Library. In recent years millions of pounds have been spent on restoring and cleaning the stonework of the colleges and university buildings. Today this great seat of learning, designed by the likes of Christopher Wren and Nicholas Hawksmoor, looks as good as it did when they created it.

A stroll through Oxford's streets reveals much of the city's history, not least its role in the English Civil War. Oxford was the Royalist headquarters as well as the seat of Charles I's parliament. Even Hitler is associated with Oxford. He was so impressed by his interpretation of its culture and sense of tradition that he planned to make it his capital once he had successfully invaded Britain.

Walk 8

Walk 8

Walk 8 Directions

① Start at the **Carfax**, where four streets converge – Carfax comes from the Latin *quadrifurcus*, for 'four-forked'. Carfax Tower is where Charles II was proclaimed King in 1660. Walk ahead into **St Aldates** and head for the entrance to **Christ Church**, Oxford's largest college, founded in 1525 by Cardinal Wolsey. When he was disgraced it was refounded as King Henry VIII's College. Later it became known as Christ Church when the college and the cathedral became one. Over the years Christ Church has had many notable students, including three Prime Ministers – Robert Peel, William Gladstone and Lord Salisbury. John Wesley, Lewis Carroll and W H Auden also studied here. The steeple is believed to be the first ever built in this country. Leave Christ Church by the south exit and walk straight ahead down the tree-lined **New Walk**. On the left is the great, green expanse of Christ Church Meadow.

WHERE TO EAT AND DRINK

There are many pubs, tea rooms and restaurants in and around Oxford. The **Turf Tavern**, off New College Lane near the Bridge of Sighs, has plenty of choice and a cosy, welcoming atmosphere.

---

② On reaching the **Thames tow path**, swing left and follow the riverbank. Keep ahead until you reach the confluence of the Thames and the **River Cherwell**. There is a steeply arched footbridge here. Avoid it and keep alongside the Cherwell. The river meanders between the meadows and sports fields. Leave the riverbank and pass through wrought-iron gates to walk up **Rose Lane**.

③ With Magdalen Bridge and Magdalen College bell tower on your right, turn left at the **High Street** or 'the High', as it is known in Oxford. Cross **Longwall Street** and turn right into **Queen's Lane**. The high perimeter wall of Queen's College is on the left and on the right are St Edmund Hall and the former parish church of St Peter-in-the-East. Continue into **New College Lane** and on the right, beyond the arch, is the entrance to **New College**. Keep along New College Lane to the **Bridge of Sighs**, a 1913 replica of its Venice namesake, and in front of you now is the **Sheldonian Theatre**.

④ Designed by Sir Christopher Wren and completed in 1669, the theatre was built to hold important university meetings and ceremonies. Turn left here for the Radcliffe Camera and cross **Radcliffe Square** towards Brasenose College, which probably took its name from a brazen door-knocker in the shape of a nose. Turn right into **Brasenose Lane**, then right again into **Turl Street**, cutting between Jesus College and Exeter College. Make for Broad Street and on the right is **St Giles**, where Charles I drilled his men during the Civil War. Turn left into Cornmarket Street, passing the Church of St Michael at the North Gate. Its Saxon tower is the oldest building in Oxford and originally linked the city wall and the North Gate. Return to the **Carfax**.

WHAT TO LOOK FOR

Alongside Rose Lane, the **University Botanic Garden**, established in 1621 by the Earl of Danby, is Britain's oldest botanic garden. The 8,000 species of plants, grown for both teaching and research at the university, demonstrate the plant kingdom's enormous diversity.

On to Mesopotamia

Escape the bustle of the city streets and follow the River Cherwell to Marston.
See map and information panel for Walk 8

•DISTANCE•	6 miles (9.7km)
•MINIMUM TIME•	2hrs 45min
•ASCENT / GRADIENT•	Negligible
•LEVEL OF DIFFICULTY•	

Walk 9 Directions
(Walk 8 option)

On reaching the **High Street**, turn right towards **Magdalen Bridge** (Point Ⓐ). Cross it and follow **St Clements Street**. Walk along to **London Place**, then branch left into **Marston Road**. Follow the road to Magdalen College Sports Ground and turn left immediately before it, taking a metalled path down to the River Cherwell. Follow the path to a strip of land, between the river and a mill stream, known as Mesopotamia, from the Greek for 'between rivers'.

Turn left over a bridge, then swing right on the opposite bank to enter the **University Parks**. Turn left and follow a concrete path, cross a bridge and turn immediately right at a kissing gate. Fork right, keep alongside the Cherwell and make for the **Tolkien seat**, in memory of J R R Tolkien, Professor of Anglo-Saxon at Merton College between 1925 and 1945. Cross the next bridge, following the path ahead.

Turn left at the next junction (Point Ⓑ) and then right at the next, avoiding a footbridge here. Cross a footbridge and stile and turn right, skirting a field to enter woodland. Go through a kissing gate and eventually the path reaches the entrance to **Marston Middle School**. Follow the drive and swing left just beyond the primary school. Turn right after a few paces, passing through the subway. Follow the walkway to the right, then turn left at **Oxford Road**.

Walk through **Old Marston**, veer left into **Mill Lane** and turn left for the **Victoria Arms**. Make for the far corner of the car park and follow the woodland path beside the river. Cross the **B4495** and continue on the footpath. On reaching two stiles, side by side, take the right path. Briefly it leaves the riverbank, sweeping right after a few paces, then back.

Cross the river at the next bridge and turn left, passing the Tolkien seat. Walk through the Parks, keep right at the fork and follow the path as it sweeps to the right to reach a map of University Parks. Turn left here, pass Linacre College and continue ahead along **St Cross Road**. Pass **Holywell Street** and follow **Longwall Street**, passing the garage where William Morris (1887–1963) built the prototype for the 'bullnose' Morris Oxford. Walk along to the **High Street**, turn right and rejoin Walk 8 at Point ③.

Godstow's Tale of Jealousy

Take a walk across ancient grazing land to Britain's greatest river.

•DISTANCE•	4¾ miles (7.7km)
•MINIMUM TIME•	1hr 45min
•ASCENT / GRADIENT•	Negligible
•LEVEL OF DIFFICULTY•	
•PATHS•	Meadow paths and tracks, tow path, road (can be busy)
•LANDSCAPE•	Ancient grazing land north west of Oxford city
•SUGGESTED MAP•	aqua3 OS Explorer 180 Oxford
•START / FINISH•	Grid reference: SP 487094
•DOG FRIENDLINESS•	Under control on Port Meadow – on lead if cattle about
•PARKING•	Public car park at Lower Wolvercote
•PUBLIC TOILETS•	At car park

Walk 10 Directions

From the car park keep right and walk through **Lower Wolvercote**. Pass between the houses and on to the **Red Lion** and the **White Hart**. Pass **Home Close** and **Rowland Close**, followed by the local post office. Continue to **Elmthorpe Road** and at this point turn right, passing through the gate to reach **Wolvercote Common**. Approach the railway and, 50yds (46m) before it, swing slightly right, following a grassy path out towards **Port Meadow**. The path gradually curves away from the line, heading for a cobbled bridge over a ditch.

Maintain the same direction across this breezy, open ground and look for barges and sailing boats gliding along the distant Thames. Look for

a gate over to the left and pass through it to a kissing gate. Keep right at the junction beyond it and right again at the next track. Head south through **Burgess Field Nature Park** to rejoin the open ground and follow a concrete track along the edge of Port Meadow.

Head towards a car park and turn right just before it at a kissing gate. Follow the bridleway to a wide footbridge over the Thames, turn right to a second footbridge and cross to the opposite bank, heading upstream now beside **Bossom's Boatyard** and Medley Sailing Club. Continue on the **Thames Path**, passing a turning to the **Perch** at Binsey, and on to **Godstow Lock**. Ahead are the remains of Godstow Abbey where, according to legend, the body of Fair Rosamond, the beautiful mistress of Henry II, was buried after she had been murdered by a jealous queen.

All that is left of Godstow Abbey is a walled enclosure with, in one corner, the shell of a 16th-century chapel. The abbey was founded in

---

WHERE TO EAT AND DRINK ⓘ

Wolvercote has a number of pubs, most of them serving a range of traditional food and drink. The **Perch** at Binsey and the **Trout** at Godstow both have a wide choice of dishes.

1139, and the nunnery here was where Rosamond de Clifford was sent by her father to finish her education. But fate took a hand. Henry II spotted Rosamond one day after she had been picked to work in a local high-class brothel – now the famous Trout Inn, one of Oxfordshire's most famous pubs.

WHILE YOU'RE THERE ℹ️

Covering 345 acres (140ha), the ancient common of **Port Meadow** is where the Freemen and Commoners of Oxford can graze geese, horses and cattle. The grazing arrangements were mentioned in the Domesday survey of 1086.

Henry was so taken with Rosamond that he installed her as his mistress in his royal palace at Woodstock, where Blenheim Palace now stands (▶ Walk 22). She even bore him two sons – William Longspee, Earl of Salisbury, and Geoffrey who became Lord Chancellor of England. The house was secret, surrounded by a maze to protect Rosamond from Henry's queen, the formidable Eleanor of Aquitaine. However, Eleanor discovered what was going on and set about getting rid of Rosamond. She managed to penetrate the maze, which was shaped like a knot, and poisoned the woman who had become a rival for her husband's affections.

Or did she? Tradition has it that Rosamond was murdered but it's possible that she escaped death and retired to Godstow to become a nun, before dying, probably from natural causes, in 1176. Her tomb was found there. As for Eleanor, she was an extremely unpopular queen and there were many people who were eager to see her discredited. Historians believe that if she did manage to find her way through

the maze, it was thanks to a clue provided by a silken thread. Some sources suggest that, confronting Rosamond finally, Eleanor forced her to drink the poison.

After Rosamond's death, royal endowments paid for silk curtains draped around the tomb and there were continuous prayers for her soul. But Bishop Hugh of Lincoln rejected such indulgence and ordered her remains to be removed. However, on his departure, the nuns concealed the bones in a perfumed leather bag, depositing them in a lead coffin in the Chapter House. Years later, the famous antiquarian John Leland recorded that when the coffin was opened, it was found to have a sweet smell.

WHAT TO LOOK FOR ℹ️

As you return to the car park look for a **memorial** on the wall by the road to two members of the Royal Flying Corps. They met their deaths in a monoplane crash just to the north of this site in September 1912. The stone was erected as a tribute to the bravery of these two British officers.

The nunnery was eventually dissolved in the mid-16th century, passing into the hands of George Owen, Henry VIII's physician. In the Civil War it was garrisoned for Charles I but seized in 1646 and almost completely destroyed by order of the Puritan commander, Colonel Fairfax. Little remains of the place now, but with a little imagination you can picture a young girl who enthralled an adulterous king, walking by the placid waters of the Thames.

Continue ahead, keeping to the left of the ruins to the road. Turn right here and pass the famous **Trout Inn** before returning to the car park.

Myths of the Rollright Stones

From Chipping Norton to an ancient site associated with a charming legend.

•DISTANCE•	8 miles (12.9km)
•MINIMUM TIME•	4hrs
•ASCENT / GRADIENT•	295ft (90m) ▲ ▲ ▲
•LEVEL OF DIFFICULTY•	🚶 🚶 🚶
•PATHS•	Field paths and tracks, country roads, 9 stiles
•LANDSCAPE•	Rolling hills on the Oxfordshire/Warwickshire border
•SUGGESTED MAP•	aqua3 OS Explorer 191 Banbury, Bicester & Chipping Norton
•START / FINISH•	Grid reference: SP 312270
•DOG FRIENDLINESS•	Under control or on lead across farmland, one lengthy stretch of country road and busy streets in Chipping Norton
•PARKING•	Free car park off A44, in centre of Chipping Norton
•PUBLIC TOILETS•	At car park

BACKGROUND TO THE WALK

Commanding a splendid position overlooking the rolling hills and valleys of the north east Cotswolds, the Rollright Stones comprise the Whispering Knights, the King's Men and the King Stone. These intriguing stones are steeped in myth and legend.

Mystical Theories

It seems a king was leading his army in this quiet corner of Oxfordshire while five of his knights stood together conspiring against him. The king met a witch near by who told him he would be King of England if he could see the settlement of Long Compton in seven long strides. As he approached the top of the ridge a mound of earth suddenly rose up before him, preventing him from seeing the village and so the king, his soldiers and his knights were all turned to stone.

In reality the Rollright Stones form a group of megalithic monuments created from large natural boulders found near the site. The stones are naturally pitted, giving them astonishing and highly unusual shapes. The five Whispering Knights are the remains of a Portal Dolmen burial chamber, probably constructed around 3800–3000 BC, long before the stone circle. It is the easternmost burial chamber of this kind in Britain. The King Stone stands alone and apart from the others, just across the county boundary in Warwickshire. The 8ft (2.4m) tall single standing stone was almost certainly erected to mark the site of a Bronze-Age cemetery which was in use around 1800–1500 BC.

All the King's Men

Finally, you come to the King's Men Stone Circle – a ceremonial monument thought to have been built around 2500–2000 BC. There are over 70 stones here, but it has been said they are impossible to count. Originally there were about 105 stones forming a continuous wall except for one narrow entrance. The King's Men Stones are arranged in an unditched circle about 100ft (30m) across and ranging in size from just a few inches to 7ft (2m). Here and there the stones are so close they almost touch.

It is not clear what the stone circle was used for but it may well have had some significance in religious and secular ceremonies. Between 200 and 300 people can fit within the circle, though it is not known how many people would attend these ceremonies or what form they took. Most mysterious of all is why this particular site was chosen. Many visitors to the Rollright Stones have questioned their origin over the years but they remain a mystery. Appropriate for such a legend as this, the remote hilltop setting of these timeless stones has more than a hint of the supernatural about it.

Walk 11 Directions

① Follow the **A44** downhill. Pass **Penhurst School**, then veer right,

through a kissing gate. Skirt the left-hand edge of the recreation ground and aim for a gate. Descend to a bridge and, when the path forks, keep right. Go up the slope to

WHERE TO EAT AND DRINK ⓘ

Chipping Norton offers a variety of pubs, hotels and tea rooms. Try the rambling old **Blue Boar** with its views of the Market Place and the town's many historic buildings and a good choice of dishes, including Gloucestershire sausages and baked rabbit. The **Black Horse** at Salford offers the chance to stop off for refreshment during the walk.

three stiles and keep ahead along the right edge of the field. Make for a gate and drop down to some double gates in the corner.

② Cross a track just beyond the gates and walk towards **Salford**, keeping the hedge on the left. Continue into the village and soon turn right by a patch of grass and a sign, 'Trout Lakes – Rectory Farm'.

③ Follow the track to a right-hand bend. Go straight ahead here, following the field edge. Make for a gate ahead and turn right in the next field. About 100yds (91m) before the field corner, turn left and follow the path across to an opening in the boundary. Veer left, then immediately right to skirt the field. Cross a little stream and maintain your direction in the next field to reach the road.

WHILE YOU'RE THERE ⓘ

Have a look at **Chipping Norton**, or 'Chippy' as the locals call it. One of the gateways to the Cotswolds, the town prospered as a result of the wool trade. The church, though not prominently situated in the town, is impressive.

④ Turn left, then left again for **Little Rollright**. After visiting the church, retrace your steps to the **D'Arcy Dalton Way** on the left. Follow the path up the field slope to the road. Cross over and continue

on the way between fields. Head for some trees and approach a stile. Don't cross it; instead, turn left and skirt the field, passing close to the **Whispering Knights**.

⑤ On reaching the road, turn left and visit the site of the **Rollright Stones**. Return to the Whispering Knights, head down the field to the stile and cross it to an immediate second stile. Walk ahead along a grassy path and turn right at the next stile towards **Brighthill Farm**. Pass alongside the buildings to a stile, head diagonally right down the field to a further stile, keep the boundary on your right and head for a stile in the bottom right corner of the field. Make for the bottom right corner of the next field, go through a gate and skirt the field, turning left at the road.

WHAT TO LOOK FOR ⓘ

The **manor house** at Little Rollright was once important. It was the home of William Blower who gave St Philip's Church its pinnacled tower in 1617. The church, which dates mostly from the 15th century, has two 17th-century monuments to the local Dixon and Blower families.

⑥ Keep right at the next fork and head towards the village of **Over Norton**. Walk through the village to the T-junction. Turn right and, when the road swings to the left by **Cleeves Corner**, join a track signposted 'Salford'. When the hedges give way, look for a waymark on the left. Follow the path down the slope, make for two kissing gates and then follow the path alongside a stone wall to reach the parish church. Join **Church Lane** and follow it as far as the T-junction. Turn right and return to the town centre.

Adlestrop to Chastleton

From a timeless village to an age-old house.

•DISTANCE•	4 miles (6.4km)
•MINIMUM TIME•	2hrs
•ASCENT / GRADIENT•	427ft (130m) ▲▲ ▲ ▲
•LEVEL OF DIFFICULTY•	棋 棋 棋
•PATHS•	Meadows, lanes, woodland, 8 stiles
•LANDSCAPE•	Low rolling hills north of Chipping Norton
•SUGGESTED MAP•	aqua3 OS Explorer OL45 The Cotswolds
•START / FINISH•	Grid reference: SP 241271
•DOG FRIENDLINESS•	Some road walking; not permitted in Chastleton House
•PARKING•	Car park (donations) beside village hall, Adlestrop
•PUBLIC TOILETS•	None on route

BACKGROUND TO THE WALK

The walk starts in the sleepy village of Adlestrop. It was not always so quiet, for trains used to stop here. The poet Edward Thomas (1878–1917) wrote a wistful little verse in which he recalled stopping here unexpectedly on the express train, apparently in the middle of nowhere, and listening to the birdsong. Set in deep, lush countryside, Adlestrop still feels well off the beaten track. Its houses are a pleasing harmony of old and new, stone roofs alternating with thatch, and cottage gardens to die for.

Chastleton House
One of the finest Jacobean mansions in England, Chastleton House stands on the hillside above its village, aloof and self-contained. The house has a magical stillness about it. It was built between 1603 and 1618 by a local wool merchant, Walter Jones, on land purchased from Robert Catesby, one of the Gunpowder plotters. Unusually, the house was to be occupied for the next 400 years by the same family.

Time-worn Perfection
The handsome grey-stone frontage of the house, with its tall windows and symmetrical gables and staircase towers, can be seen clearly from the road. If you want to see inside, however, you are urged to book ahead, for opening hours and numbers are strictly limited. Chastleton is no grand showplace and, since its recent acquisition, the National Trust has been careful to conserve the house in its peaceful, time-worn perfection, rather than attempt to restore it to some former glory. There is a panelled hall and an ornate great chamber and, on the top floor, a vast long gallery with plastered ceiling looks out over the gardens. Much of the furniture is original and the chambers are richly adorned with embroideries, quilts and tapestries.

Chastleton may have led a quiet life, but hardly a dull one. A secret room above the parlour was used to hide a fugitive in the Civil War. Arthur Jones was a Royalist, and had fought for the King – and lost – at the Battle of Worcester in 1651. He fled to his father's house at Chastleton and was forced into the hiding place when a party of soldiers arrived in hot pursuit. Arthur's wife, Sarah, was obliged to put them up for the night. This resourceful woman laced their ale with laudanum and, while his pursuers snored, Arthur made his escape. He was able to return at the Restoration and planted an oak in the grounds to celebrate his narrow escape.

Croquet on the Lawn

The formal gardens at Chastleton are contemporary with the house, its lawns studded with dark topiary. It is sometimes claimed that croquet was invented here. In fact, the game had been around for centuries, but was only introduced to England in 1852. The rules of the game were set out for the first time here at Chastleton in 1865.

Walk 12 **Directions**

① From the car park in Adlestrop turn left on to the road and left again up a broad track, signposted 'Macmillan Way'. Climb a stile by a gate and enter a meadow. Bear left by a yellow waymarker. Walk up the field, with **Fern Farm** up to your right. Cross a stile in the top left corner and continue up the fence. Soon cross a stile to your left and continue up the same line, passing a bulging oak tree on your right. Cross another stile and continue straight ahead up the field. The hill gets steeper.

Walk 12

② Cross a stile by a wooden gate and walk up through the line of trees. Continue straight across the next field. Go over the crest of the hill and through an iron gate, into the **Chastleton Estate**. Continue straight ahead up an avenue of trees. Go through two gates to reach the road.

WHAT TO LOOK FOR ⓘ
Walking into the green ring of **Chastleton Barrow** is an eerie experience. Surrounded by a bank or rampart planted with trees, it clearly functioned once as a defensive site, most probably in the Iron Age. An ancient track linked the camp with the Rollright Stones (► Walk 11). This wide grassy amphitheatre on the hilltop is now used to hold cattle.

③ Turn right and walk along the road, passing **Chastleton House** on your left, then **St Mary's Church**. Pass the arcaded dovecote on the right. Stay on the road, which bends up right, and pass a car park on your right.

④ Where the road bends sharply right, turn left into a private road. Cross a cattle grid and immediately turn right. Go through a gate and take the bridleway diagonally left up the field, parallel with the road. On a level with **Barrow House farm**, go through a small gate, cross the drive and take the left of two gates opposite. Go through two more gates to enter the tree circle of **Chastleton Barrow**.

⑤ When you have seen the barrow, retrace your route to the drive and turn left. At the road turn left. After a short distance turn right across a stile. Walk ahead through the trees and follow the path, which leads diagonally left across the field, with

WHILE YOU'RE THERE ⓘ
The walk offers excellent views across to the busy market town of **Stow-on-the-Wold**, reached along the A436. Perched on the very edge of the Wolds, it is known to catch any blast of wind, and can be icy in winter – hence the local saying, 'Stow-on-the-Wold, where the wind blows cold.' This is antique-hunter's heaven, however, and there's a steady flow of visitors to explore the shops, whatever the season.

views to Stow-on-the-Wold. Keep straight on down, passing some barns to your left. Cross a track and walk ahead down the edge of woodland. At the bottom corner bear right into the woods. Follow the winding path, cross a stile and emerge at a field.

⑥ Turn left along the track. Turn right before you reach the gateway, and walk down the edge of the field. Go through a gate into the **Long Drive**. Follow this path through the trees and emerge on to the road. Cross over, go through a gateway on the other side and soon turn right along a narrow footpath. Follow this through the trees; cross a stile and turn left along the road. Take the first turning left and walk through **Adlestrop** village, keeping right to return to the car park and the start of the walk.

WHERE TO EAT AND DRINK ⓘ
The venerable villages of Lower Oddington and Upper Oddington offer an appealing diversion on your way to Stow-on-the-Wold and are served by two good pubs. The **Fox** at Lower Oddington is set opposite a beautiful little manor house. Continue through the villages to reach the **Horse and Groom** at Upper Oddington, which describes itself as a village inn and has the bonus of a big car park behind.

A Right Royal Scandal at Cumnor Place

Explore the countryside surrounding a village that is the setting for a centuries-old mystery.

•DISTANCE•	6 miles (9.7km)
•MINIMUM TIME•	2hrs 30min
•ASCENT / GRADIENT•	Negligible ▲▲▲
•LEVEL OF DIFFICULTY•	👫 👫 👫
•PATHS•	Field paths, quiet lanes and tracks, 1 stile
•LANDSCAPE•	Fields and pasture adjacent to River Thames
•SUGGESTED MAP•	aqua3 OS Explorer 180 Oxford
•START / FINISH•	Grid reference: SP 458044
•DOG FRIENDLINESS•	On lead in villages and on country lanes
•PARKING•	Spaces by village hall in Cumnor
•PUBLIC TOILETS•	None on route

BACKGROUND TO THE WALK

Sadly, a stone fireplace set in a bank in an Oxfordshire churchyard is virtually all that is left of Cumnor Place, the setting for a mystery that has baffled historians for centuries. The manor of Cumnor was once owned by Abingdon Abbey and the remains of the house, the abbot's summer residence, form part of the extended parish churchyard. Cumnor Place, which stood to the west of the church, was demolished in 1810 by the Earl of Abingdon.

So what exactly happened here so long ago? What was it that scandalised Elizabethan England? Following the Dissolution, the house was leased by Anthony Forster, the steward of Lord Robert Dudley, Queen Elizabeth's favourite.

The Tale of Dudley and Amy

Dudley, third son of the Earl of Warwick, married Amy Robsart in 1550. She was the only daughter of a wealthy Norfolk landowner and it seems likely the couple met when Dudley travelled with his father to East Anglia to quell a local rebellion. Amy was young when she married, only 18, but the couple seemed happy together – at least on the face of it. However, three years later Dudley found himself in the Tower of London, charged with conspiring to prevent Mary Tudor from getting her inheritance. He was later pardoned and resumed life on his father-in-law's estates in Norfolk.

A Change of Circumstances

The death of Mary in 1558 and the accession of Elizabeth to the throne had a significant impact on Dudley. He and the new Queen had been friends since childhood and now they had the opportunity to become even closer. Elizabeth was certainly smitten – it is said she smiled on no-one as she smiled on Dudley.

While her husband spent much of his time away at court, Amy stayed with friends in the country. She was lonely without him and there were rumours that she was ailing. Whispers of Dudley's close friendship with the Queen would not have helped matters.

In 1560 Lady Dudley went to stay with Anthony Forster and his wife at Cumnor Place. On Sunday 8 September she died after falling downstairs and breaking her neck.

On hearing the news at court, Dudley allegedly showed no outward signs of grief or distress, perhaps fearing that the circumstances surrounding his wife's death would damage his reputation. The main question was 'what caused her death?' Was it suicide, natural causes, a tragic accident or, worst of all, murder? If so, did Dudley plan it and was Forster involved? He knew that if Dudley were free to marry the Queen, then his own future would be assured.

Nothing was proved, nor has it ever been. The matter was investigated fully and the jury returned a verdict of 'mischance or accidental death'. But was it? Though the Queen didn't marry Dudley, within three years of Amy's death she made him Earl of Leicester.

Walk 13 Directions

① Turn right from the parking area and walk along to the mini-roundabout. Turn right into **Appleton Road** and pass the **Bear and Ragged Staff** pub on the right. Veer half left just a few paces beyond it and join a footpath signposted to Bessels Leigh. Pass the **cricket club** on the left and continue on the track. When it peters out continue ahead in the field, keeping a ditch on your right. Pass alongside a line of trees on the far side of the field, turn left, then turn right and make for an opening in the corner, concealed by vegetation in summer. Go straight on to a galvanised gate and keep some houses over to the left beyond the pasture. Cross a footbridge to a galvanised gate, swing left and cross the field towards the road. Keep in line with telephone wires and make for a waymark in the field corner. Follow the drive to the road.

WHERE TO EAT AND DRINK ⓘ

The **Bear and Ragged Staff**, which is the emblem for the Earls of Warwick and the county emblem for Warwickshire, lies on the edge of Cumnor. Food is available and there is a popular beer garden. The **Greyhound** at Bessels Leigh serves food all day. The **Thatched Tavern** at Appleton offers food and a beer garden. The **Eight Bells** at Eaton is handy for snacks and more substantial fare.

---

② To visit the **Greyhound** pub, turn left. To continue the walk turn right and follow the road through **Bessels Leigh** and continue out in the countryside, cutting between farmland. On reaching a junction, keep left to the next junction. Go straight on into the village of **Eaton** and pass the **Eight Bells** pub.

③ Follow the lane out of Eaton and through flat countryside. When it becomes enclosed by trees, look for a view of the Thames on the left. Continue to **Bablock Hythe** and look across the river to the

Ferryman Inn. Walk back along the lane for a few paces and turn left at the bridleway signposted 'Cumnor'.

④ Pass through a gate and when, some time later, the path curves to the left, look for the **Physic Well** in the trees to the left of your route. This is a muddy spring which was once greatly valued as a source of healing waters. Emerge from the trees and cut between fields towards pylons. Go through a gate, join a drive and walk ahead. Ignore the turning to **Upper Whitley Farm** and continue into **Cumnor**, passing **Leys Farm** on the right. Look for the United Reformed church and return to the **village hall**.

WHAT TO LOOK FOR

As you enter Eaton by road from Bessels Leigh, look for a **memorial stone** by the entrance to West Farm. The stone recalls that the trees here were given by staff and friends of A Howard Cornish MBE JP (1895–1964), County Alderman and lifelong farmer here. Near it is a Victorian postbox. Look for the letters VR – Victoria Regina.

WHILE YOU'RE THERE ⓘ

Pause and savour the peace and tranquillity of **Bablock Hythe**. The 19th-century writer Matthew Arnold knew this place well and made references to Bablock Hythe and the surrounding countryside in his work. It was his 'Scholar Gipsy' who 'oft was met crossing the stripling Thames at Bablock-hythe.' The Romans crossed the river here and a ferry has been in service on and off for more than 1,000 years.

A Woodland Detour to Appleton

Extend the walk to look at a classic brick and stone village.
See map and information panel for Walk 13

•DISTANCE•	7 miles (11.3km)
•MINIMUM TIME•	2hrs 45min
•ASCENT / GRADIENT•	Negligible
•LEVEL OF DIFFICULTY•	

Walk 14 Directions (Walk 13 option)

Turn left at the sign for Appleton and go through the galvanised gate (Point Ⓐ). Follow the track/road to the right and straight along to two sets of galvanised gates and some farm outbuildings on the right Continue across the pasture to a kissing gate leading into **Bessels Leigh Wood**.

This area has been continuously wooded for over 400 years but has recently been altered by a process of partial planting of non-native species. These days, the woodland is managed for quiet recreation and wildlife, and the timber growth will be managed to take full advantage of this resource for the future. Birch and oak are among the trees to be found here, while sycamore is the result of planting in the 1950s. Roe, fallow and muntjac deer are known to inhabit the woods.

Pass a stile and footpath on the right and continue ahead through the wood. Emerging from the trees, cut across a footbridge and follow a straight path between fences and pastures. Cross a stile and footbridge and approach **Appleton church**. Pass to the side of it to the drive and follow it into the village. Follow **Church Road** to the T-junction and turn right opposite the post office and stores (Point Ⓑ).

Appleton is a picturesque village of brick and stone houses. The manor house is partly 12th-century, one of the oldest in the county, and its Norman doorway is still visible over the churchyard wall. The church is essentially Norman with a 15th-century tower and some later additions. Inside is a tomb to a lord of the manor, a member of the Fettiplace family, who was knighted by Queen Elizabeth when she visited Woodstock.

Walk along to the **Thatched Tavern** and then head out of Appleton, passing the village sign. Just a few paces beyond the entrance to a house called **Hengrove**, turn left at a footpath sign for Eaton. Follow the track as it sweeps to the right and skirts the field, keeping alongside the boundary. Join a clear track on a bend and continue ahead. Pass some farm outbuildings to reach the road at **Eaton**, rejoining Walk 13 at this point.

Walk 15

Stonesfield Slate Sculpting

Find out what a pretty village has in common with Oxford's colleges.

•**DISTANCE**•	3½ miles (5.7km)
•**MINIMUM TIME**•	1hr 30min
•**ASCENT / GRADIENT**•	164ft (50m) ▲ ▲ ▲
•**LEVEL OF DIFFICULTY**•	🚶 🚶 🚶
•**PATHS**•	Riverside path, tracks and roads (can be busy)
•**LANDSCAPE**•	Undulating country bisected by River Evenlode
•**SUGGESTED MAP**•	aqua3 OS Explorer 180 Oxford
•**START / FINISH**•	Grid reference: SP 393171
•**DOG FRIENDLINESS**•	On lead in Stonesfield and along road on return leg
•**PARKING**•	Spaces in village centre
•**PUBLIC TOILETS**•	None on route

Walk 15 Directions

Stonesfield is a hilly village closely associated with the tradition of slate mining. The stone is a type of Jurassic limestone known as 'pendle'. It's a little-known fact outside Oxfordshire, but many of the stone roofing slates used in this part of the county come from Stonesfield, as do the slates of many Oxford colleges. The slate was reputedly the best, lightest and least porous of roofing materials, with the local stone pits and slate quarries dating mainly from the 16th century.

The village is known for a charming winter-time tradition dating back to when slate mining was the main

WHAT TO LOOK FOR ⓘ
Parts of this walk in the Evenlode Valley are a sheer delight, especially where the route crosses the **Evenlode**, described by Hilaire Belloc – an energetic walker, writer and politician, who attended Balliol College, Oxford – as 'a lovely river, all alone … forgotten in the western wolds.'

industry in the area. When a sharp frost was expected, the church bells would toll, often in the middle of the night, reminding the residents of Stonesfield of the need to ensure that the stone was immediately uncovered and exposed to the elements. This was not part of some bizzare rural custom. There was method in their madness.

When the villagers rose from their beds in the morning, they would discover that the freezing temperature had split the stone neatly into layers which could then be sculpted into slates. The Romans, who constructed several villas near Stonesfield during their occupation, probably quarried stone in the district. The village has expanded hugely over the years but the centre of Stonesfield, in the vicinity of the church, still has a great deal of charm and character, retaining an evocative hint of the past.

The last pit at Stonesfield closed before the First World War, and the last slate miner died in the 1940s. Today, the inhabitants of the village earn their living in other ways, many of them working in nearby Oxford. Demand for replacement slates is now met using materials from demolished buildings.

With the church over to the right, leave Stonesfield by heading south. Pass rows of houses and, when the road turns sharp right at **Churchfields**, go straight on into **Brook Lane**. Follow the unmade road, pass a turning to the **Rectory** on the right and lines of bungalows on the left and continue down towards the **River Evenlode**. Ahead of you arc glimpses of a rolling, well-wooded landscape in the valley below. Descend a series of steps, following the sunken path to the riverbank.

WHERE TO EAT AND DRINK ⓘ

The **Black Head** at Stonesfield offers meals and snacks, including sandwiches, beefburgers and steak-and-kidney pudding. A popular beer garden adds to the attractions. The nearby towns of Charlbury, Chipping Norton, Witney and Woodstock offer a wide range of inns and tea rooms.

Cross the river via the footbridge and keep heading south, following the bridleway across the fields. The Evenlode can be seen over to the right, snaking through the countryside. Pass through a gate and then turn immediately right to follow a waymarked path alongside the river. The walk cuts through margins of vegetation and undergrowth before the outline of a railway bridge looms into view ahead. Pass under the bridge and follow the path as it runs close to the water's edge. In places, the boughs of the trees reach down to touch the surface of the Evenlode. Beech trees line the bank along

here, and soon the river sweeps away to the right.

On reaching the road, walk along to the junction and turn right for **Stonesfield**. Cross the Evenlode and pass some roadside dwellings. Pass over the railway line, then turn immediately left for Fawler and Charlbury. Follow this road for about ½ mile (800m). Further on, a curtain of woodland can be seen in the distance, draped spectacularly across the valley – one of many scenic highlights on this walk.

Turn right by a cottage and head up the track towards the stone outbuildings of **Oaklands Farm**. Keep right at the buildings, following the track round the east side of the farm. Head north on the track, across open country, with views of Stonesfield in the distance. The track bends right before passing a copper beech tree. Soon you reach the road.

Turn left and then right by some stone barns and industrial units. Continue along the lane into **Stonesfield**, keeping right at the next junction. Head up to the next junction and turn right by a plaque commemorating 60 glorious years of Queen Victoria. Pass **Peaks Lane** and continue between stone houses and cottages. Curve left beyond the Methodist church and walk along **High Street**. Soon you reach the church where the walk began.

WHILE YOU'RE THERE ⓘ

Visit the fully excavated **North Leigh Roman Villa**, a short drive to the south of Stonesfield. The site is close to the Evenlode and is a fine example of a Roman villa with a good mosaic pavement. The Roman road known as Akeman Street crosses the river here.

Churchill and Cornwell

A walk linking two intriguing villages on the D'Arcy Dalton Way.

•DISTANCE•	5½ miles (8.8km)
•MINIMUM TIME•	2hrs 30min
•ASCENT / GRADIENT•	459ft (140m) ▲▲ ▲ ▲
•LEVEL OF DIFFICULTY•	👫 👫 👫
•PATHS•	Open farmland, village lanes, quiet roads, 12 stiles
•LANDSCAPE•	Broad, open valley once used by a railway line
•SUGGESTED MAP•	aqua3 OS Explorer OL45 The Cotswolds
•START / FINISH•	Grid reference: SP 270270
•DOG FRIENDLINESS•	Some road walking, otherwise good
•PARKING•	Lay-by beside phone box at Cornwell
•PUBLIC TOILETS•	None on route

BACKGROUND TO THE WALK

There's a slightly theatrical air about Cornwell, as if this neat and charming village were poised and waiting for the next act, or a film camera to roll. It huddles on one side of a small valley, smugly holding on to its secrets, for, as part of the Cornwell Manor Estate, it is private and inaccessible. You may look, but not touch. The manor itself, where owner Peter Ward and his family live today, is carefully screened from prying eyes, except for the lovely stone front, which boldly faces up to the road from behind its high, wrought-iron gate.

Cornwell

Cornwell's best known secret is that it was thoroughly remodelled just before the Second World War by the architect-cum-salvage king, Clough Williams-Ellis (1883–1978). Born in Northamptonshire, Williams-Ellis developed an eclectic design style that mixed architectural details in a particularly flamboyant way. By the time he was working on Cornwell, his own pet project at Portmeirion in North Wales – what he called his home for fallen buildings – was already well established. The then owner of Cornwell, Mrs Anthony Gillson, employed Williams-Ellis to modernise the village, but also to create the magnificent terraced gardens at the manor, along with other alterations including the addition of a ballroom. His influence may be clearly seen on the village hall (originally the school), with its bowed end and eccentric chimney stack-cum-bellcote.

The little Church of St Peter remained untouched at this time, though the handsome wooden candelabras are attributed to the style of Clough Williams-Ellis. It dates back to Norman times, and its position away from the village, in fact on the opposite side of the manor, is curious. It is believed that a village once surrounded the church, but disappeared during the ravages of the plague years.

Churchill

In direct contrast to Cornwell, the attractions of Churchill are both up-front and open to view. The tower of All Saints' Church dominates the skyline for miles around and, if it looks strangely familiar to you, that's probably because it's a scaled-down model of the tower of Magdalene College, Oxford. As the choristers of that famous establishment sing from their tower to greet the dawn every May Day morning, so local choristers gather at the top of All Saints' to do the same. The church was built in 1826 by James Langston, a mover and shaker in the village, and it is he who is affectionately remembered with the large and elaborate fountain next door.

Churchill boasts two famous sons. The first is Warren Hastings (1732–1818), a colourful figure who rose to become Governor-General of India, and lost his fortune in successfully defending himself against a charge of cruelty and corruption. The second is William Smith (1769–1839), who produced the first geological map of England.

Walk 16

Walk 16 **Directions**

① Turn left and walk down and up through **Cornwell**. Pass a farm, right, and turn right, signposted 'D'Arcy Dalton Way'. Where the track veers left, keep ahead, by a fingerpost. Walk down an orchard and bear left. Go right at the corner

through the hedge. Soon go through a gate on your left. Turn right and walk downhill. Cross a stile, right; follow the path down towards **St Peter's Church**.

② Go through a gate into the churchyard. Pass the church, and leave via a squeeze gate. Walk straight ahead down the hill, cross

Walk 16

the bridge at the bottom and go up to the gate. Turn right along the drive, passing **Cornwell Glebe**. Bear left along the road. Pass a turning to Salford.

③ Turn right along a bridleway, signed 'Kingham'. Follow this for ½ mile (800m), then cross a stile on the left and walk ahead down the field edge. Cross a footbridge and follow the path diagonally right. Cross another footbridge and bear right along the stream. Soon bear left and cross a stile. Cross the track. Cross a footbridge opposite, and bear diagonally right up the field. Cross a footbridge in a hedge and continue on this line through another hedge.

WHERE TO EAT AND DRINK

The pub in Churchill was closed at the time of writing. It's therefore worth making your way westwards to Bledington, where the venerable **King's Head Inn** looks out on the huge village green, with its streams and tiny bridges. In a beautiful setting, the pub is a free house, offering restaurant food and accommodation, with plenty of tables to sit at outside. A children's play area is near by.

next junction, then left at the end. Follow this road out of the village, passing the old chapel. Continue through **Sarsden Halt**.

⑥ Follow the road right, then keep straight ahead along the green lane. After ½ mile (800m) climb the stile on your left and bear diagonally up the field. Walk up the hedge and turn right along the road.

⑦ Continue walking straight ahead through **Kingham Hill Farm**. Pass through a gate at the other side and carry on straight across two fields. Cross a stile, then a footbridge and stile and keep straight on. Pass an old gate and continue up the field. Cross another stile and continue, bearing slightly left over the hill crest. Take the gate to the left of the main gate and turn left up the road to return to your car and the start of the walk.

WHAT TO LOOK FOR

The hamlet of **Sarsden Halt** was once a stop on the railway line – hence the appearance and railway theme of some of its buildings. The line ran along the valley floor, linking Chipping Norton in the east with the main line at Kingham Station to the west. Its route is crossed twice in the course of the walk.

④ Cross a stile into the woods. Follow the path down, over a footbridge and right up the other side. Go through a gate and ahead towards **Churchill**. Cross a stile, then bear right beside a house. Cross a stile and turn left up the road. Pass a post-box and turn right along a path. At the next road turn left. At the top turn right.

⑤ Turn right again before you reach the **church** and follow the path round the back of the old pub. Cross a stile, pass a barn and maintain your direction into a field. Soon turn right over a stile and walk down a lane. When you get to the road turn left; turn right at the

WHILE YOU'RE THERE

Chipping Norton is the highest town in Oxfordshire, its wealth built on the wool trade. It centres on a large market square, with a little town hall dating from 1835 and some handsome Georgian frontages. There are lots of opportunities for shopping and eating out. The distinctive Bliss Valley Tweed Mill with its tall Tuscan-style chimney, on the north side of town, has been converted to flats.

Wanderings at Wychwood

A gentle walk through rolling Oxfordshire farmland and a corner of an ancient forest.

•DISTANCE•	5¾ miles (9.2km)
•MINIMUM TIME•	2hrs 30min
•ASCENT / GRADIENT•	574ft (175m) ▲▲▲
•LEVEL OF DIFFICULTY•	🚶🚶 🚶🚶 🚶🚶
•PATHS•	Field paths, quiet roads, woodland tracks
•LANDSCAPE•	Gently rolling hills of arable farmland, ancient woods
•SUGGESTED MAP•	aqua3 OS Explorer 180 Oxford
•START / FINISH•	Grid reference: SP 318194
•DOG FRIENDLINESS•	Lead essential for road stretches, otherwise excellent
•PARKING•	On village street near phone box, Chilson
•PUBLIC TOILETS•	None on route

BACKGROUND TO THE WALK

The Wychwood takes its name from a local Saxon tribe, the Hwicce. At the time of the Norman conquest, Wychwood Forest was one of four royal hunting grounds in England, and covered most of western Oxfordshire. The leafy remains of this once magnificent demesne are now mostly confined to the hilltops that lie between Ascott-under-Wychwood, Charlbury, Ramsden and Leafield, and private land ownership means that access for walkers is sometimes frustratingly limited.

A National Nature Reserve

At its heart is a National Nature Reserve, which preserves some 360 species of wild flowers and ferns, including the elusive yellow star of Bethlehem and the bizarre toothwort, a parasitic plant that is found on the roots of some trees. This walk takes you through the edge of the old woodland, on a path that in spring is carpeted with vivid drifts of bluebells, which stretch away under the trees as far as the eye can see. The rich variety of wild flowers means a corresponding abundance of butterflies, including peacock, tortoiseshell and orange tip.

The Shrinking Forest

By 1300 the once-flourishing 'forest' had been split into three sections: Woodstock, based around the royal hunting lodge first built there during the reign of Ethelred II; the area around Cornbury Park; and a section around Witney, where the Bishop of Winchester had built his palace. The forest continued to decline and, by 1857, only some 10 square miles (26sq km) were left to be removed from Forest Law by an act of parliament. As the enclosure of land became commonplace in the 1860s, Kingstanding Farm, passed on this walk, was one of seven new farms built at this time to take advantage of the newly available land.

The Ascott Martyrs

The village of Ascott-under-Wychwood is tucked in the valley below the remnants of the Wychwood, along with its near neighbours Shipton-under-Wychwood and Milton-under-Wychwood. Ascott may not be the prettiest of these Cotswold villages, but it has another claim to fame: the Ascott Martyrs. These 16 young women played their part in the Agricultural Revolution of the 19th century when, in 1873, they attempted to dissuade Ramsden men from taking over the jobs of local men, who had been sacked for membership of the Agricultural Workers' Union. Indeed, the women were accused of encouraging the imported labourers to join the same union.

The announcement of their punishment – imprisonment with hard labour – caused a riot outside the court in Chipping Norton and the women had to be secretly transferred to Oxford gaol. Their sentences were later remitted by Queen Victoria and some accounts say that she sent each woman a red flannel petticoat and five shillings. The union presented them with blue silk to make dresses and £5 each. These bold women are remembered with a bench on the village green.

Walk 17 Directions

① From the phone box, turn south along the village street, and right up **School Lane**, passing various houses and the **Old School** at the end, on the right. Follow the path straight on into the field ahead, with the hedge to your right. Stay on the path round the edge of the field as it kinks left then right. Keep straight on, descend steadily, and follow as the track bends right.

At the hedge turn right then immediately left through a gateway; take the track diagonally left across the field towards Ascott-under-Wychwood, to meet a lane.

② Turn left along the lane through **Ascott d'Oyley**, passing **Yew Tree Farm** on the right. Beyond d'Oyley House, and just before a recreation ground, turn left up a track, **Priory Lane**, which becomes a grassy footpath. This bends sharp right, and emerges at a road by a house. Turn left up the road, and cross the main road at the top with care. Continue straight ahead up the lane, signed 'Leafield'. Follow this straight uphill for a mile (1.6km), to pass through the buildings of **Kingstanding Farm**.

WHERE TO EAT AND DRINK ⓘ
The old **Swan** pub lies near the railway station and opposite the Holy Trinity Church in the western part of Ascott-under Wychwood. It serves Morrells ales, and offers home-cooked food all day and a beer garden. On Mondays the pub takes on the vital role of post office, when pensions are served over the bar instead of pints.

③ Continue down the stony track and keep straight on. It leads along the bottom of a winding, secret valley, with the solid spire of Leafield church up to your right. Emerge at a main road; turn left and follow the road as it snakes uphill, with **Wychwood Forest** to your right. After about 1 mile (1.6km) the road descends into woodland. As it ascends again, look for a wooden gate on the left, signed 'Circular Walk Footpath'.

④ Turn left through here and follow the path up the edge of the woods. Keep right and cross the

WHILE YOU'RE THERE ⓘ
Look out for **guided nature walks** run by the Wychwood Project, which was set up to raise modern awareness and appreciation of the Wychwood. The project takes account of the fact that a hunting forest traditionally included meadows and farmland as well as wooded country, and identifies with the landscape between Taynton and Woodstock, and from just south of Chipping Norton all the way down to Northmoor. For information check their website: www.wychwoodproject.org

clearing of **Stag's Plain**. Bend left and right and continue on the path through the woods, carpeted with bluebells in spring.

⑤ Start to descend and emerge from the woods. Continue straight ahead, following the track downhill, with a hedge on your right. Pass **Smallstones Farm**, over to the left. Bend left at the bottom of the field, cross a stile, and take the path that leads to the left, down the hill and past **Chilson Hill Cottage** (right).

⑥ At the bottom of the drive turn right along the main road and immediately left down the road that leads into **Chilson** village. Enter the village and keep straight on past the tiny triangular green, passing the old **Primitive Methodist chapel** on your left. Pass the end of **School Lane** and return to your car.

WHAT TO LOOK FOR ⓘ
We were surprised by a loudly buzzing brown mass, hanging from a broken elder branch beside the track – a swarm of **honey bees**, looking for a new home before the summer. It recalled the old saying: 'A swarm of bees in May is worth a load of hay, A swarm of bees in June is worth a silver spoon, But a swarm of bees in July isn't worth a fly.'

Walk 17

A Final Folly in Faringdon

Visit an intriguing Gothic tower before venturing into open countryside.

•DISTANCE•	7½ miles (12.1km)
•MINIMUM TIME•	3hrs
•ASCENT / GRADIENT•	115ft (35m)
•LEVEL OF DIFFICULTY•	
•PATHS•	Roads (mostly quiet), field paths, drives and tracks, 15 stiles
•LANDSCAPE•	Gently rolling farmland
•SUGGESTED MAP•	aqua3 OS Explorer 170 Abingdon, Wantage
•START / FINISH•	Grid reference: SU 286956
•DOG FRIENDLINESS•	On lead where indicated
•PARKING•	Long stay car park off Gloucester Street, Faringdon
•PUBLIC TOILETS•	Southampton Street car park

BACKGROUND TO THE WALK

Britain's follies are fascinating, their exuberance and eccentricity often reflecting the character of those who built them. A typical example is Gerald Tyrwhitt-Wilson, 14th Lord Berners (1883–1950), whose name alone conjures up images of the stereotypical upper-class twit or chinless wonder immortalised in old, much-loved British comedy films.

Widely regarded as Britain's last major folly tower and very much a local landmark, Faringdon Folly dates back to 1935. While out walking on Folly Hill one day, Lord Berners turned to his companion, Robert Heber-Percy, and commented that the hill would look even better with a folly built on it. Berners was far from conventional and those who knew him were rarely surprised by anything he said or did. He was, in every sense of the word, a gay lord – colourful, generous, talented, amusing and unmarried. Berners embodied all the characteristics of the classic British eccentric – sadly lacking in today's world. Typically, whatever he did was characterised by a dash of mischief.

Aside from his sense of fun and dry mocking humour, Berners was one of life's naturally gifted players. He was an accomplished writer, painter and composer – Stravinsky called him the best British composer of the 20th century and Diaghilev commissioned him to compose the score for the ballet *Triumph of Neptune*. During his time at Faringdon House, he hosted many glittering parties and among his regular guests were some of the most talented figures of the pre-war arts world.

Word quickly spread that Berners was planning to build on the hill, provoking strong opposition among neighbouring landowners. Berners won his battle, however, and completion of the 100ft (30m) tower was marked by a spectacular party and firework display on 5 November. Berners released hundreds of doves dyed red, white and blue.

Faringdon Folly is a curious mix of styles. Berners commissioned his friend Lord Wellesley to build the tower, choosing a Gothic design which the architect deplored. While Berners was abroad, Wellesley began construction work, but when his client returned he discovered the tower bore no resemblance to his specification. Instead it followed classical lines, with not a hint of its creator's flamboyant personality to be seen. Berners immediately ordered that the tower be completed in ornate Gothic. Robert Heber-Percy, who lived with Lord Berners at Faringdon House, gifted the tower to the town of Faringdon in 1983.

Walk 18

Walk 18 **Directions**

① Follow the car park exit road and turn left at the T-junction. Make for the town centre, following **Gloucester Street** along to **Cornmarket**. Pass the Red Lion and the Bell pubs, cross the **Market Place** by keeping to the right side and pass the **Folly** pub. Turn right into **Stanford Road**, then left at the sign for Folly Hill. Take the path, following it as it begins a moderate climb to **Faringdon Folly**. Keep to the right of the tower, emerge from the trees and continue ahead down the slope to a stile. Go straight ahead across the field to a stile leading out to the **A420** road.

WHAT TO LOOK FOR

As you reach the end of the walk, look out for **All Saints parish church**. The Pye Chapel recalls Henry Pye who was Lord of the Manor here when George III made him Poet Laureate.

② Cross over to a stile and a sign for Hatford and keep the field boundary on your right. On reaching a wood and some white gates, continue ahead across the field. Cross a drive leading to **Wadley Lodge** and keep ahead. Make for a white gate ahead in the boundary and keep left here, following trees and bushes along the field edge. Make for the corner and continue ahead on the bridleway, cutting across fields with woodland over to the right. This is **Hatford Gorse** and just beyond it is a dilapidated barn. Follow the

WHERE TO EAT AND DRINK

Plenty in Faringdon – pubs, including the **Bell** and the **Red Lion**; bakers or sandwich bars for snacks. The **Lamb** at Buckland has an imaginative menu.

bridleway to a house and join the road on a hairpin bend. Keep ahead to a left curve. The bridleway runs straight on, part of Walk 19.

WHILE YOU'RE THERE

Make time to explore **Faringdon**. King Alfred (► Walk 23) had a royal manor here and King John granted a charter for a weekly market. The Old Town Hall is worth a look, as are the Georgian façades of the Market Place inns.

③ Follow the lane to the **A420**, cross over and take the drive ahead towards **Barcote Park**. Turn left at the footpath sign and cross the field to two stiles in the line of trees. Cross them and turn right along the field edge for 50yds (46m) to the next stile. Go down the field and through a line of trees to two stiles and head up the slope to the next stile. Cross a sports field to a beech tree and gate. Follow the drive to the road, turn right and walk through the village of **Littleworth**.

④ As the road bends sharp right by **Hill House**, go through the gate marked **Chapel House**, signposted 'Church Walk and Faringdon'. Follow the track to the right for a few paces to a stile and gate. Take the path west across the field, with Faringdon Folly in the distance. Look for farm outbuildings ahead, with a fence now on the right. Cross a stile, keep to the right of the buildings, negotiate two stiles with a track in between and walk ahead. Make for gates in the field corner, continue ahead in the next pasture and approach a house. Keep to the right of it, cut between fields and fences, go through a farm gate and follow a track to the outskirts of **Faringdon**. Continue ahead on the road and round to the **Market Place**. Return to the car park.

The Beauty of Buckland

Visit a picturesque village dominated by a splendid 18th-century house.
See map and information panel for Walk 18

Walk 19

•DISTANCE•	10 miles (16.1km)
•MINIMUM TIME•	4hrs
•ASCENT / GRADIENT•	115ft (35m)
•LEVEL OF DIFFICULTY•	

Walk 19 Directions (Walk 18 option)

As the road bends left (Point Ⓐ), walk ahead along the bridleway, following it across the fields towards trees and the semi-wooded slopes of a **golf course**. Join an enclosed path running between fairways and pass through a gate into the mixed woodland. Cut between laurels and look for a monkey puzzle tree on the left. On reaching a field enclosed by trees, with thick woodland on your right, turn left and pass to the side of a galvanised gate. Continue ahead on the bridleway and, further on, you reach the former outbuildings of **Home Farm**, recently converted into private dwellings (Point Ⓑ).

On the right is an octagonal dovecote, which has also been given a new lease of life. Keep ahead on the drive to the busy **A420** road. Cross over to a footpath sign, gate and lodge. Walk ahead for a few paces to a stile, then go diagonally right across the field. Buckland House can be seen in the distance. Cross a stile and follow the path through woodland to the road. Turn left into **Buckland**, passing the **Lamb** pub on the left.

On reaching a T-junction (Point Ⓒ), go straight over to visit the **Church of St Mary the Virgin**, which contains various manorial box pews, hatchment boards and brasses, and an alabaster carving of the Adoration of the Shepherds. Return to this point, turn right towards Witney and immediately pass the Roman Catholic church.

Beyond it is a very good view of Buckland House, built by the Throckmorton family in the mid-18th century. With its central block of mellow stone and octagonal pavilions at either end, one formerly a chapel and the other a library, the house is a perfect example of neoclassical architecture. The estate includes a large lake and a deer park of 150 acres (61ha). Buckland House is not open to the public.

Pass the main entrance to the house and keep ahead to the T-junction. Cross over and follow a bridleway across the fields. Eventually you reach a canopy of trees. Keep ahead, following the path through the grounds of **St Hugh's School**. Look for hard tennis courts and a ha-ha before reaching the road. Turn right, then left just beyond **Rushey Cottage**, joining a bridleway which cuts across the fields. Join the drive to **Barcote Park** and rejoin Walk 18.

The Ewelme Chaucers

A downland walk to an historic church associated with a famous poet's family.

Walk 20

•DISTANCE•	4 miles (6.4km)
•MINIMUM TIME•	1hr 30min
•ASCENT / GRADIENT•	164ft (50m)
•LEVEL OF DIFFICULTY•	
•PATHS•	Farm tracks, paths and roads (can be busy in Ewelme)
•LANDSCAPE•	Spectacular downland
•SUGGESTED MAP•	aqua3 OS Explorer 171 Chiltern Hills West
•START / FINISH•	Grid reference: SU 648912
•DOG FRIENDLINESS•	On lead in Ewelme, under control near livestock
•PARKING•	Small car park by sports ground at Ewelme
•PUBLIC TOILETS•	None on route

Walk 20 Directions

Turn right out of the car park and follow the road between trees and hedgerows towards Swyncombe and Cookley Green. Cross over at the next junction and follow the bridleway between stone pillars and wrought-iron and gilt gates towards **Down Farm**.

Keep to the main track, following it for about ½ mile (800m). Pass the farm outbuildings and continue between trees and hedgerows. Turn left at an intersection, about ¼ mile (400m) from the farm, and head north, skirting a field by keeping to the left-hand boundary. Follow the **Swan's Way** into the next field and continue with the hedge now on your right. There are very pleasant views along here towards distant patches of woodland.

On reaching the road, turn right and when, after a short distance, it bends right, go straight on along the edge of a pretty beechwood. This is the route of the Icknield

Way, an ancient highway. Turn left after a few paces and follow the **Chiltern Way** over open fields and downland. When the track bends right, go straight on towards farm outbuildings. Pass to the left of them and, further on, ignore some double gates on the right. Keep ahead as the track bends left and follow the path between fields to the road.

Turn left, pass the Ewelme village sign and a bridleway on the right, and make for the village centre. Cross **Hampden Way** and follow the road as it sweeps sharp right, avoiding the turning to the church. Pass **Chaucer Court** on the right and the site of the old village pound where stray horses and cattle were held. It was probably last in use immediately prior to the Second World War.

WHERE TO EAT AND DRINK

The **Shepherds Hut** is just outside Ewelme village centre. The menu includes light snacks and main meals (no food is available on Sunday evening). Outside there is a large beer garden.

Walk 20

Turn left at the T-junction towards Swyncombe and Crowmarsh, passing a pond on the left. This is Ewelme **High Street**. Just before the road bends sharp right, turn left into **Burroughs Hill** and begin a moderate but brief climb to Ewelme churchyard and the road.

WHAT TO LOOK FOR ⓘ
Beside the path to the Old Rectory, adjoining the church, is the **grave of Jerome K Jerome**, who is best known for his wonderful book about a Thames journey, *Three Men in a Boat* (1889).

Among the village's most historic and distinctive buildings is the early 15th-century church, St Mary's, which featured in the television filming of John Mortimer's *Paradise Postponed*. Step inside and have a look at the church's many treasures before finishing the walk.

As you enter the church, look for the altar tomb which lies in St John's Chapel between the first and second bays of the chancel. The tomb is that of Thomas Chaucer, who died in 1434, and his wife Matilda Burghersh, who died two years later. Thomas was the son of Geoffrey Chaucer, the poet, and his mother was Philippa Roet, whose sister was the third wife of John of Gaunt, son of Edward III.

The marble slab is decorated with the brasses of Thomas in plate armour, with the unicorn crest at his feet. In each corner is a shield of arms. On the sides of the tomb is one of the largest and most fascinating displays of medieval shields of arms to be found anywhere in the country. The shields and the inscription were restored in 1843 and are thought to date back to the 1430s.

Another imposing tomb in the church is that of Alice, Duchess of Suffolk. Daughter of Thomas and Matilda, Alice died in 1475. Almost certainly the tomb was erected in the church soon after her death.

Alice inherited the manor of Ewelme from her mother and, after marrying William de la Pole, the Duke of Suffolk, she and her husband planned to transform Ewelme into a model medieval village. However, the Duke did not live to see the fruits of his labour – his reputation had been flawed by accusations of corruption and impropriety and he had made many enemies along the way.

WHILE YOU'RE THERE ⓘ
Allow time to look round **Ewelme**. The village is renowned for its watercress beds which once yielded a sizeable harvest. A leisurely tour of Ewelme's quiet streets and hidden corners reveals an assortment of architectural styles.

In 1450, while on his way to France, the Duke was brutally murdered. His widow took charge of the work at Ewelme, supervising the building of the school and almshouses and the rebuilding of the church. When Queen Victoria became Sovereign of the Order of the Garter, it was uncertain as to where a lady should wear the garter. To try and resolve the matter, it was decided to inspect the tombs of those who wore the Garter. Among them was the effigy of the Duchess of Suffolk. Alice is depicted wearing the Order of the Garter on her left wrist.

After visiting the church, turn right and pass the **Old Rectory**. Continue down the lane and out of the village. Cross over at the next junction, back to the car park.

Blenheim Palace Parkland

A fine walk in peaceful countryside to one of Britain's top country houses.

•DISTANCE•	7 miles (11.3km)
•MINIMUM TIME•	3hrs
•ASCENT / GRADIENT•	150ft (46m) ▲ ▲ ▲
•LEVEL OF DIFFICULTY•	🚶 🚶 🚶
•PATHS•	Field paths and tracks, parkland paths and estate drives. Some quiet road walking, 3 stiles
•LANDSCAPE•	Farmland and parkland
•SUGGESTED MAP•	aqua3 OS Explorer 180 Oxford
•START / FINISH•	Grid reference: SP 411158
•DOG FRIENDLINESS•	On lead in grounds of Blenheim Palace
•PARKING•	Spaces in centre of Combe
•PUBLIC TOILETS•	Blenheim Palace, for visitors; otherwise none on route

BACKGROUND TO THE WALK

When King George III first set eyes on Blenheim Palace, he remarked, 'We have nothing to equal this.' Few would disagree with him. The views of the palace, the lake and the Grand Bridge from the waterside path on this delightful walk are stunning. Set in a magnificent 2,000-acre (810ha) park landscaped by 'Capability' Brown, the great Baroque house covers a staggering 7 acres (2.8ha) and is England's largest stately home.

Blenheim Palace took nearly 20 years to build and was finally completed in 1722. The architect John Vanbrugh was commissioned to design the house for John Churchill, 1st Duke of Marlborough (1650–1722), following his victory over the French at Blenheim in 1704. Inside, there are various state rooms and tapestries, the Long Library – considered by many to be the finest room in the house – and the room where Winston Churchill was born in 1874 (► Walk 22).

A Just Reward

It was Queen Anne who decided that John Churchill's efforts in battle should be suitably rewarded, reflecting the high regard in which the nation held him. But what exactly did Churchill do to earn such respect? As a soldier and as a statesman, he was responsible for supressing Louis XIV's grand imperialist ambitions in Europe. His spirit and determination resulted in a crushing and humiliating defeat of the French at Blenheim on 13 August 1704. Though he had achieved his objective, Churchill was not ready to retire from the battlefield and he went on to secure many more victories in his illustrious career.

In gratitude, Queen Anne conferred the Royal Manor of Woodstock on the Duke of Marlborough and his heirs in perpetuity, and a sum of £500,000 was voted by parliament for the building of Blenheim Palace. But problems lay ahead. The Duke's wife, Sarah, was Princess Anne's favourite companion before she became Queen in 1702. Sarah used her close friendship and her influence in royal circles to secure a dukedom for her husband, and it was she, not the Duke of Marlborough, who approved the plans and then supervised the building work. Proving just how ruthless and determined she could be, Sarah rejected Sir Christopher Wren's designs in favour of those produced by John Vanbrugh.

Walk 21

A Sweet House

The Duchess remained a thorn in the side of builders and architects for some time, insisting that all she wanted was a 'clean, sweet house and garden, be it ever so small.' Parliament complained about the spiralling cost, money gradually ran out and the Duchess forbade Vanbrugh from seeing the finished building in 1725, refusing him entry to the grounds.

Characterised by ornament and exuberance, creating a memorable skyline, Blenheim Palace – decidedly not 'ever so small' – is not to everyone's taste, though the immense scale of the house has to be seen as a tribute to the skill and ingenuity of its creators. The vast parkland and gardens, too, are renowned for their beauty and range. Vanbrugh's Grand Bridge is the focal point, but elsewhere there are formal water terraces and an arboretum – among many other features.

Walk 21 Directions

① From the green, take the road signposted 'East End'. Swing right by the village pump into the churchyard and keep to the left of the church. Exit through the gap in the boundary wall, flanked by two gravestones, and begin skirting the right-hand edge of the sports field. After about 50yds (46m), branch off into the trees, then head diagonally across the field. Cross into the next

---

WHERE TO EAT AND DRINK ℹ

Refreshments are available at **Blenheim Palace** – the Indian Room Restaurant serves full lunches and afternoon tea, the Water Terrace buffet offers a wide selection of hot and cold food, and the Pleasure Gardens Cafeteria has a self-service buffet. Sandwiches and drinks are available from the Country Kitchen. The **Cock Inn** is a pleasant village local. Expect a range of beers and a selection of snacks and main courses.

---

field and keep to the right edge of the wood. In the next field, turn left, still with trees on the left, and go up the slope to the woodland corner. Pass through a gap in the hedge and cross the field.

② Exit to the road, turn left and keep right at the next junction. Walk along to **Combe Gate**. Go through the large kissing gate into the grounds of **Blenheim Palace**, keep left at the junction and follow the drive through the parkland. As it sweeps left to a cattle grid, veer off to the right by a sign 'visitors are welcome to walk in the park'. Follow the grassy path to a stile. Keep right when the path divides and walk beside the western arm of **The Lake**.

③ Eventually you reach a tarmac drive. Turn right and walk down towards the **Grand Bridge**. As you approach it, turn sharp left, passing between mature trees with **Queen Pool** on your right. Cross a cattle grid and keep ahead through the park. With the **Column of Victory** on your left, follow the drive as it sweeps to the right.

④ Turn left at a cattle grid, in line with the buildings of **Furze Platt** on the right. Join the Oxfordshire Way, cross a stile and follow the grassy track alongside trees, then between fields. At length cross a track and continue towards woodland. Enter the trees and turn left after a few paces to join a clear track running through the wood.

⑤ After about 150yds (137m) take the first left turning, crossing a footbridge to reach the edge of a field. Keep right here, following the obvious path across the fields. When you reach a track, turn right. Keep alongside trees to a junction. Turn right and follow the track down through a wood and diagonally left across a strip of pasture to an opening in the trees. Go up to a track and cross it to a ladder stile.

⑥ Turn left to a hedge, then turn right, keeping it and a ditch on your right. Skirt a field to the road, turn right and walk back into **Combe**.

WHAT TO LOOK FOR ℹ

The **Column of Victory** dates back to 1731 and was built to commemorate the heroic efforts of the 1st Duke of Marlborough on the battlefield. Until the mid-19th century, this famous landmark was home to one of the last pairs of breeding ravens in the county.

WHILE YOU'RE THERE ℹ

Have a look at **Combe church**. The original building, which was in the valley about 1 mile (1.6km) from its present site, was built during the Norman period. The present church was built or rebuilt in about 1395, about 50 years after the villagers moved their homes up the hill out of the valley. The design of the church is a prime example of the Early Perpendicular style, with a stone pulpit and medieval stained glass. Unusually, the war memorial at Combe gives the dates the men of the village who lost their lives. All except one died in the First World War.

Churchill's Grave at Bladon

Take a walk to the heart of rural Oxfordshire, visiting the final resting place of Britain's most famous statesman.

•DISTANCE•	5 miles (8km)
•MINIMUM TIME•	2hrs 15min
•ASCENT / GRADIENT•	90ft (27m)
•LEVEL OF DIFFICULTY•	
•PATHS•	Field and woodland paths and tracks, quiet roads, 7 stiles
•LANDSCAPE•	Farmland and woodland on east bank of River Evenlode
•SUGGESTED MAP•	aqua3 OS Explorer 180 Oxford
•START / FINISH•	Grid reference: SP 468138
•DOG FRIENDLINESS•	Under control on farmland and on lead where requested
•PARKING•	Limited spaces outside Begbroke church, St Michael's Lane
•PUBLIC TOILETS•	None on route

BACKGROUND TO THE WALK

One name remains synonymous with Britain's victory over the Nazi regime in 1945 – that of Sir Winston Churchill. And yet if it had not been for the Second World War, Churchill would have been almost forgotten by now, his political record meaning little, if anything, in today's world. His shifting allegiance between the Conservative and Liberal parties might have given him a slightly higher profile, but that is all.

Instead, he came into his own as Britain's wartime leader, renowned for his inspired rhetoric and his familiar 'V for victory' salute. He so perfectly embodied the fighting spirit and determination of the British character and, as well as being a magnificent statesman, he was probably the greatest orator of modern times.

A Great Man is Born

Churchill was born at Blenheim Palace (► Walk 21) in 1874. He was educated at Harrow and Sandhurst and took part in the charge of the 21st Lancers at the Battle of Omdurman before becoming a newspaper correspondent in the Boer War. In 1900 he entered parliament as a Tory MP but later crossed the floor of the House to join the Liberal majority.

As Home Secretary he witnessed the famous Siege of Sidney Street and, as First Lord of the Admiralty, with the threat of the First World War looming, he began strengthening Britain's military arsenal, becoming Minister of Munitions in 1917. However, between the wars he found himself in the political wilderness, with his concern over the increasing Nazi threat largely ignored.

The dark days of 1940 eventually dawned and Neville Chamberlain stepped down as Prime Minister, heralding Churchill's 'walk with destiny'. Not only would this be Britain's finest hour, but Churchill's too – the zenith of his political career. During the next five years he would excel himself. He began shaping the 1941 Atlantic Charter, looked to America for help and support in the war and masterminded the strategy adopted for the Battle of Britain, Alamein and the North African campaign. With the war finally won, a victorious Churchill went to the country, hoping for a landslide result. But it was not to be. He lost the election to Labour.

Churchill's Last Years

In 1951, six years after losing the election, Churchill was returned to power. He won the Nobel Prize for Literature in 1953, but had quite a severe stroke in the same year. With Britain's post-war recovery well advanced, he eventually retired as Prime Minister in 1955, his health by now in dramatic decline. He died ten years later, and at the express wish of the Queen was the first commoner since Wellington to be afforded a state funeral. Churchill's death not only represented the passing of a momentous era but came to be acknowledged as the end of the British Empire.

Seventy years earlier, aged 20, Churchill wrote to his mother: 'I went this morning to Bladon to look at Papa's grave ... I was so struck by the sense of quietness and peace, as well as by the old-world air of the place, that my sadness was not unmixed with solace...'

Walk 22 Directions

① Keep the church behind you, walk along to **Spring Hill Road** and turn right. Follow the lane through two sharp bends, passing **Hall Farm**. Avoid the path on the right and continue ahead to a stile and some galvanised gates. Follow the track up a gentle slope and on to the next stile and a cattle grid. Keep ahead, passing a stone-built house on the left, and then swing right across the field, passing under telegraph wires. Pass into the next field and turn right.

② Follow the obvious boundary across several fields, eventually turning left in the corner. Continue for about 50yd (46m) and look for a stile and footbridge on the right. Keep ahead in the next field, with the hedge on the left. On reaching the field corner, go forward for a few paces, then turn right through an opening in the hedge into the adjoining field. Maintain the same direction as before, with the boundary on your left. Make for a stile and oak tree in the field corner. Continue ahead across the next field, keeping to the left edge of woodland. With trees hard by you on the right, follow the path towards **Burleigh Lodge**. Swing left for a few paces to a stile leading out to the road.

WHILE YOU'RE THERE

Have a look at Bladon's parish **Church of St Martin**. There has been a church on this site for over 800 years. The place oozes history – Henry II and Thomas Becket walked together here, Edward the Black Prince grew up here and Elizabeth I was imprisoned near by.

---

③ Turn right by the millennium stone, pass the lodge and walk along the road to a footpath sign on the right for Bladon. Cross the stile and keep the hedge on the left. Make for a footbridge in the field corner, turn left and follow the hedgerow. Look for a hedge running diagonally right, keep it on your left and head towards the rooftops of Bladon. Make for a stile leading out to the road on a bend. Go forward, keep the entrance to the **Lamb** pub car park on the left, continue to the next junction and cross over to

Church Street. Walk along to the **Church of St Martin** and head through the churchyard to the gate on the far side.

④ Turn right and follow the tarmac lane to some wooden gates. Continue ahead on the field path to the corner and turn right at the waymark. With a hedgerow on the left, pass to the left of woodland and head for a white gate, with the road beyond. Turn left by some lock-up garages and follow the path signposted to Begbroke.

WHERE TO EAT AND DRINK

The **Royal Sun** at Begbroke, a few minutes on foot from the start and finish of the walk, offers traditional Sunday lunches, main meals and snacks. The **Lamb** at Bladon, midway round the circuit, also includes a good range of hot and cold dishes and beers.

---

⑤ Cross a rectangular pasture and, at the far end, follow the path into the trees and through a gate. Emerge at length from the wood at another gate and continue ahead along the field boundary towards Begbroke. Go through a gate in the corner and follow the path alongside the drive to the road. Turn left and left again into **St Michael's Lane**, returning to the church.

WHAT TO LOOK FOR

Visitors from all corners of the world visit **Churchill's final resting place** at Bladon, expressing their gratitude and admiration for the leadership qualities of this legendary statesman in the visitor book and on his grave. 'Thank you for showing the world how to stand up to tyranny,' wrote an American woman from Virginia the day I was there. 'May Sir Winston never be forgotten. RIP' was another heartfelt message.

Alfred's Greatness Remembered at Wantage

Visit the statue of a revered British king before heading for spectacular downland country.

•DISTANCE•	6 miles (9.7km)
•MINIMUM TIME•	2hrs 45min
•ASCENT / GRADIENT•	150ft (46m)
•LEVEL OF DIFFICULTY•	
•PATHS•	Pavements, tow path, field paths and tracks, 1 stile
•LANDSCAPE•	Town outskirts, farmland and downland
•SUGGESTED MAP•	aqua3 OS Explorer 170 Abingdon, Wantage
•START / FINISH•	Grid reference: SU 397881
•DOG FRIENDLINESS•	On lead on town outskirts, in villages and if horses about
•PARKING•	Long-stay car park off Mill Street
•PUBLIC TOILETS•	By Town Council offices off Church Street and Portway

BACKGROUND TO THE WALK

King Alfred (AD 849–99) is one of those heroic figures we may remember from the pages of school history books. His victories in battle and his reputation for scholarship and justice rightly earned him the title Alfred the Great. He is suitably commemorated in the Market Place of Wantage, the town of his birth. The striking marble statue of him at its centre was sculpted by Count Gleichen, Prince of Hohenlohne-Langenburg, and unveiled in 1877. As you pass by it, in the initial stages of the walk, note the battleaxe in one hand and manuscript in the other.

Alfred Makes his Mark

Alfred, the youngest son of King Aethelwulf, succeeded his brother Aethelred as King in AD 871, at a time when Viking invaders had overwhelmed most of England to the north of the Thames and Wessex was under constant attack. Seven years later Alfred defeated the Danish army at Edington in Wiltshire. He repelled another invasion in 885 and captured London the following year.

Alfred is also remembered for building a fleet, which earned him a reputation as 'father of the English navy,' and creating a ring of fortified strongholds around his kingdom. He was an educated man and as a child he travelled to Rome and to the Frankish court of Charles I, the Bald. He played a key role in reviving and translating many documents and was instrumental in codifying the laws of his kingdom. For example, he made a treaty which recognised the partition of England, with the Danelaw under Viking rule.

A Mighty Battle

But it is the Battle of Ashdown, not far from Wantage, fought in AD 871, with which most local people probably associate Alfred. While the Danes held Reading, it was Alfred's intention to try and entice them away from the river, which they commanded, and confront them on the downs.

Alfred and his brother Aethelred successfully encouraged the enemy to pursue them up the Kennet Valley. The two men then fell back towards the downs with the Danes in hot pursuit. Then, at Ashdown, they stood their ground. What happened next is not clear. The area surrounding the Ridgeway here was guarded by forts and perhaps Alfred looked to them for help in his quest for victory.

Walk 23

Alfred Wins the Day

Whatever took place high on the downs above Wantage, Alfred won the day, sending the Danes packing with the hollow sound of defeat ringing in their ears. Above all, Alfred had taught them a lesson, proving that once they were away from their boats they were an easy target. Alfred scored a number of victories over the Danes before being forced to retreat to the relative safety of the Somerset Marshes. However, he had taken a positive first step in his efforts to resist the Vikings during the following years.

Walk 23 **Directions**

① Keep to the right edge of the car park and look for the pedestrian exit. Turn left into **Mill Street** and walk up into the **Market Place**. Make for the statue of King Alfred and then follow the signs for the museum. Approach the parish Church of St Peter and St Paul and turn left into **Church Street**. The museum is opposite you at the next junction. Turn right here, avoid Locks Lane and follow **Priory Road** to the left. Head for **Portway** and cross over to a footpath to the left of **The Croft**.

WHERE TO EAT AND DRINK   ⓘ

There's a good selection of pubs around Wantage. The **Greyhound** at Letcombe Regis offers a wide selection of home-cooked food and a large garden. Freshly made baguettes, sandwiches and home-made pies feature on the menu. Refreshments are also available at the **Vale and Downland Museum**.

---

② Follow the clear tarmac path as it runs between fences and playing fields. At length you reach a housing estate; continue ahead into **Letcombe Regis** and make for the junction with Courthill Road. Keep it on your left and go straight ahead through the village, passing the **Greyhound** pub and a thatched cottage dated 1698.

WHAT TO LOOK FOR   ⓘ

The **Wilts and Berks Canal** was opened in 1810, connecting the Kennet and Avon canal and the Thames. The canal was eventually closed in 1914, though much of the route still survives. Restoration work is taking place and it is hoped that, some time during the 21st century, boats will once more glide along the entire length of this waterway.

---

③ Turn right by the church, signposted 'Letcombe Bassett and Lambourn' and, when the road bends sharp left, go straight ahead. After a few paces the drive bends right. Keep ahead along a path between banks of vegetation, following it as it curves right, then swings left. Pass **Antwicks Stud** over to the right and climb gently between trees and bushes.

WHILE YOU'RE THERE   ⓘ

The **Vale and Downland Museum**, in Wantage, describes itself as the starting point for exploring the Vale of White Horse. The museum is very informative, explaining in great detail the history of the region and how it has been shaped and influenced over the centuries.

---

④ Turn right at the next intersection and follow the tree-lined track to the road. Turn left and make for the junction. Cross over, pass alongside a house and follow **Cornhill Lane**. Begin a gentle descent, cross a track and continue down the slope. Avoid the right turning and keep ahead to a footbridge crossing the old Wilts and Berks Canal. Turn right and follow the tow path.

⑤ Cross the **A417** road and continue towards Wantage. Follow a drive and then take the parallel path on the right, running alongside a section of restored canal. On reaching a tarmac drive, turn right and walk along to a row of houses. Turn left at the path junction, pass a recreation ground and follow the path as it curves right. Turn left into **Wasborough Avenue**, then, after some lock-up garages, left into **St Mary's Way**. Turn right and swing left into **Belmont**. Keep right at the fork and make for **Mill Street**. Keep left and the car park is on the left.

Letcombe Bassett

Visit a pretty village disguised in print by one of Britain's greatest writers.
See map and information panel for Walk 23

·DISTANCE·	8½ miles (13.7km)
·MINIMUM TIME·	3hrs 30min
·ASCENT / GRADIENT·	150ft (46m) ▲▲ ▲ ▲
·LEVEL OF DIFFICULTY·	🚶 🚶 🚶

Walk 24 Directions (Walk 23 option)

Turn left at the crossroads (Point Ⓐ) by **Letcombe Regis church** (signposted 'village and downs only'). When the road bends left, swing right at a bridleway sign and make for a gate and footpath waymark. Avoid them and keep left, after a few paces arriving at a junction of rights of way. Keep right here, following the sign for the nature trail. Ignore the stile on the left and follow the path between fence and hedge. Pass a gate leading to the nature trail and follow the delightful tree-shaded path above the **Letcombe Brook**. Cross a stile and eventually the path drops down to the road (Point Ⓑ). To visit the village of **Letcombe Bassett**, turn left, otherwise turn right and go down the hill.

For many years Letcombe Bassett has been closely associated with racehorse training, with strings of horses often seen making their way to the nearby gallops or in the surrounding lanes. The growing of watercress in the Letcombe Brook is also a local tradition, and Letcombe Bassett has a strong literary connection.

Thomas Hardy based the village of Cresscombe on this settlement in his classic novel *Jude the Obscure*, first published in 1895. Arabella's Cottage is where Jude, hiking over the downs, stumbles on his future wife washing pig's chitterlings in the local stream. She attracts Jude's attention by lobbing part of the pig at him, signalling the beginning of Jude's downfall. Hardy selected other nearby towns and villages to appear in the story. Fawley and Wantage became Marygreen and Alfredston respectively, and Oxford (► Walk 8) was thinly disguised as Christminster.

Letcombe Bassett is also associated with another writer. Jonathan Swift, who wrote *Gulliver's Travels*, visited the village in 1714 at the invitation of the rector. It is said he occupied his time writing under a mulberry tree in the Old Rectory garden.

Pass a thatched cottage (Point Ⓒ) and turn left just beyond it, signposted 'Childrey'. Follow the bridleway between the fields and at length you come to a junction with a track known as **Green Road**. Turn right and pass a path running off sharp left, followed by a right of way on the right. Continue on Green Road and rejoin Walk 23 at the next junction.

Ardington – Country Estate

This delightful walk makes for a village that was once a centre for cloth.

•DISTANCE•	5½ miles (8.8km)
•MINIMUM TIME•	1hr 45min
•ASCENT / GRADIENT•	164ft (50m)
•LEVEL OF DIFFICULTY•	
•PATHS•	Bridleways, field paths and quiet roads, 3 stiles
•LANDSCAPE•	Open landscape at foot of downs and Ridgeway
•SUGGESTED MAP•	aqua3 OS Explorer 170 Abingdon, Wantage
•START / FINISH•	Grid reference: SU 431884
•DOG FRIENDLINESS•	On lead in villages, under control between
•PARKING•	Free car park at Loyd-Lindsay Rooms in Ardington
•PUBLIC TOILETS•	None on route

Walk 25 Directions

The village of Ardington, with neighbouring Lockinge, forms part of a large self-contained country estate established in the 19th century by landowner Robert Loyd-Lindsay. He fought in the Crimea, was one of the recipients of the Victoria Cross and later became Baron Wantage. Loyd-Lindsay resigned from the army to farm the Lockinge Estate, a wedding present from his father-in-law, a wealthy banker.

During the next few years, Loyd-Lindsay rebuilt Ardington and Lockinge as model villages, formed a co-operative selling good-quality food, and became one of this area's great agricultural pioneers, creating an enterprising business. A *Daily News* reporter wrote of the estate:

WHERE TO EAT AND DRINK ⓘ

Try **Cobwebs Tearoom** at Ardington for light refreshments. The 400-year-old **Boar's Head** has a reputation for good food. The **Wheatsheaf** at East Hendred is one of several pubs in the village.

'It is a little self-contained world in which nobody is idle, nobody is in absolute want, in which there is no hunger or squalor.'

In 1944 the 18,000-acre (7,290ha) estate passed to Christopher Loyd, son of Lady Wantage's cousin. To help clear death and estate duties amounting to £500,000, Loyd ordered the Wantage's old home, in whose gardens 50 men once worked, to be demolished. He also sold 8,000 acres (3,240ha), a number of cottages and many art treasures, and moved to a smaller house near by.

However, not all has been lost. The social, economic and political climate may have changed since Baron Wantage's day, but there have been determined efforts in recent years to try and ensure that the estate continues to survive. Many of the old farm outbuildings have been converted into craft shops, workshops, offices, a picture gallery and a pottery, helping to boost the local economy, raise the village's profile and provide much-needed employment for local people.

Next door to Ardington, Lockinge has been a venue for point-to-point meetings for 50 years. Nationally, Lockinge is one of the few courses where the original turf remains, giving perfect, fast-draining going. The undulating landscape is ideal too, providing spectators with a natural amphitheatre. Many famous names in the world of racing are associated with Lockinge. The late Princess Margaret and Her Majesty Queen Elizabeth the Queen Mother attended the Easter Monday meeting in 1957, watching their horse Gipsy Love finish second in the Open race.

WHILE YOU'RE THERE

Take a walk through **East Hendred**. In the 16th and 17th centuries, the village was closely associated with cloth-making and a fair took place annually along the Golden Mile, stretching as far as the Ridgeway. Many of the timber-built houses and thatched cottages in East Hendred date from that period.

From the car park turn right and pass the shop and tea room. Turn right just beyond them into **Church Street** and, when the road curves right, turn left at the 'no horses and ponies' sign. Pass through a brick arch and follow the path to the road opposite a timber-framed cottage. Turn right, pass a turning on the left and keep left at the next intersection of tracks.

Note the 'farm vehicles only' sign. Pass the buildings of **Red Barn** and, when the farm track bends right, go straight on along a grassy path between fields and through trees to reach a stile, crossing **Ginge Brook**. Pass **West Hendred church** and cross the road to a stile and a sign for East Hendred. Cross the field, keeping the fence and trees on the

right-hand side, to the next stile and cross a track, following the bridleway between fences towards East Hendred.

On reaching the outskirts of the village, pass between houses and bungalows and follow **Horn Lane** down to the junction. To visit the village centre and the church, turn left. To continue the walk, turn right. Pass **St Mary's Road** and a house called **Monks Orchard** on the left. **Monks Farm House** lies on the right. Go up the slope between trees, pass a turning to **Hendred Farm** on the left, and then turn right immediately beyond a belt of woodland. Follow the byway in a straight line alongside the trees and, once clear of them, keep ahead between fields.

Cross a road and continue on the next section of byway, following the edge of the field down to **Ginge Brook**. Cross the brook to a track and keep ahead between fields. On reaching the road on a bend, go forward and then round to the right, towards **Ardington House**. Cross the **Ardington Brook**, pass the church and turn immediately right. The entrance to Holy Trinity Church is on your right-hand side, just before you get to the **Boar's Head**. Pass the entrance to Ardington House on the right and make for the junction. Turn left and return to the car park.

WHAT TO LOOK FOR

Ginge Brook helped the villages of East and West Hendred achieve prosperity. It powered watermills, not only to grind corn, but also to work fulling mills for beating and fulling the cloth that was manufactured in this area. The brook was also used in the process of soaking flax to make the fibres soft enough to spin.

Walk 26

Witney – from Town to Country

Discover Witney's many treasures before heading for a popular country park on the town's outskirts.

•DISTANCE•	3½ miles (5.7km)
•MINIMUM TIME•	1hr 30min
•ASCENT / GRADIENT•	Negligible
•LEVEL OF DIFFICULTY•	
•PATHS•	Pavements, meadow and waterside paths, 1 stile
•LANDSCAPE•	Urban, country park and waterside on town outskirts
•SUGGESTED MAP•	aqua3 OS Explorer 180 Oxford
•START / FINISH•	Grid reference: SP 357096
•DOG FRIENDLINESS•	Busy streets at start and finish. Under control or on lead in Witney Lake and Meadows Country Park
•PARKING•	Public car park by Woolgate Shopping Centre, off Witan Way
•PUBLIC TOILETS•	Woolgate Shopping Centre, recreation ground and Cogges Manor Farm Museum (for visitors)

BACKGROUND TO THE WALK

Unlike Burford and Broadway, Witney never established itself as a Cotswold honeypot. Perhaps it is just as well. It is a place to stumble on, to be discovered without the fuss of coach parties and souvenir hunters. Stroll through its picturesque streets and you'll find a great deal of charm and character. It is attractive without being twee, smart without being 'touristy'. In short, it is classic Middle England. One of Witney's best views is from Church Green, looking across to the parish church at the southern end. This quiet corner of the town has the feel of a small English cathedral city and if Witney were ever descended upon by tourism marketing men, the focus of their attention would surely be here.

Witney's Famous Blankets

Perhaps the main reason the town never became a major attraction is its industrial past. During the Middle Ages Witney became the centre of a thriving woollen trade. It was the famous Cotswold sheep and the meandering River Windrush that contributed to the town's success – the river proved to be eminently suitable for the scouring of the woollen cloth. Fortunately, the townsfolk knew how to yield the best from these attributes and in later years Witney became famous throughout the world for producing blankets.

It was in 1669 that Richard Early apprenticed his teenage son, Thomas, to the woollen trade. The boy lived up to his father's expectations and by 1688 he was one of the town's leading master weavers. He was so successful that he was chosen to present a pair of gold-fringed blankets to James II. In 1711 the Witney weavers were granted a charter to form a Company of Blanket Weavers. This signifcant development, though long overdue, was welcomed by the district's weaving community, and weavers operating within a 20-mile (32km) radius of the town were required to bring their blankets to the company's headquarters to be inspected and hallmarked.

Thomas Early became the first master of the company and in later years the Early family presented blankets to King George III and Queen Charlotte as part of their royal visit to Oxfordshire in 1788. However, it wasn't long before the Industrial Revolution got under way and the wind of change began to blow through Witney, as innovative machinery ushered in a new era in the manufacturing industries. The traditional weavers feared for their jobs and riots broke out in the streets. But it was to no avail – in spite of all the protests, the new order was here to stay.

In 1960 Witney's two major blanket manufacturers merged, consolidating an association already forged by intermarriage between the two families. With the eventual closure of the company, Witney's famous tradition for producing blankets now lies at the core of the town's industrial heritage.

Walk 26 Directions

① Turn right into **Langdale Gate** and walk along towards the **Butter Cross**. Turn left immediately before

it and walk down the left side of **Church Green**. Have a look at the remains of the **Bishop's Palace** and then visit **St Mary's Church** next door. With your back to the church, walk along the left side of Church

Green and turn left at the Butter Cross into **Corn Street**. Keep ahead and, when the street becomes pleasantly tree-lined, cutting between handsome houses, turn left just beyond the **Three Horseshoes** pub into **The Crofts**. Follow the road between terraced stone houses, evoking the days when Witney was a thriving mill town.

WHERE TO EAT AND DRINK

The **Eagle Tavern** in Corn Street is one among many pubs in Witney. Expect a good and inexpensive range of meals and snacks. Alternatively, there are several cafés and restaurants in the town.

② Follow **The Crofts** to the left and turn right at the end. Keep a stone wall on the left and walk along to **St Mary's Court**. Continue ahead along an alleyway, with a school and the spire of St Mary's on the left and, when you reach the corner of a recreation ground, keep to its right edge, passing a toilet block. Turn right at the road, then turn first left at the pedestrian lights into **Station Lane**.

③ Follow the road through an industrial estate and take the path at the end, beneath the **A40**. Avoid a footbridge on the right and walk ahead through a kissing gate. The walk now cuts between **Witney Lake** and surrounding meadows,

WHAT TO LOOK FOR

Witney Lake and Meadows Country Park covers 75 acres (30ha) and includes the site of a large former gravel pit, two streams of the River Windrush and fields of hay and meadowland. Acquired by Witney Town Council in 1988, the country park is home to many different species of wildlife, including tawny owls, sparrowhawks, butterflies and damselflies.

part of a country park. Continue along the lakeside path, with the houses of Ducklington seen over to the right beyond an area of scrub. Keep **Emma's Dike** left and curve to the left. The lake is still clearly seen, as is Witney church spire at intervals in the distance. On the right is the **River Windrush**. Make for a large concrete bridge and cross it, branching left to a kissing gate.

④ Keep the field boundary over to your left and look for a kissing gate by the **A40**. Pass under it again to another kissing gate and head north to a stile, keeping your back to the main road. Cross over to a gate and keep ahead with office buildings seen on the left. Pass under power lines to two kissing gates and a notice board. Keep ahead, passing to the right of a dilapidated mill which originally had its own undershot wheels. Follow the path between margins of vegetation and eventually you reach a spur path to **Cogges Manor Farm Museum**.

WHILE YOU'RE THERE

Visit the **Cogges Manor Farm Museum**, which illustrates how this 20-acre (8.1ha) site would have looked in the Victorian era, with traditional breeds of animals, original farm buildings and displays of farm implements and machinery. Daily demonstrations of domestic and farm work take place in the manor house, dairy and farmyard.

⑤ To visit the museum, turn right and follow the path and adjoining cycleway to the Priory and St Mary's Church. Continue to the adjoining museum and then retrace your steps, heading now for Witney town centre. Pass an electricity sub station on the right and walk along to the road. Cross over into **Langdale Gate** and return to the car park.

Burford – a Classic Cotswold Town

Discover the delights of an ancient settlement with a long history on this attractive walk through the Windrush Valley.

Walk 27

•DISTANCE•	5 miles (8km)
•MINIMUM TIME•	2hrs 30min
•ASCENT / GRADIENT•	250ft (76m) ▲▲ ▲ ▲
•LEVEL OF DIFFICULTY•	🚶 🚶 🚶
•PATHS•	Field and riverside paths, tracks, country roads, 7 stiles
•LANDSCAPE•	Undulating Windrush Valley to east of Burford
•SUGGESTED MAP•	aqua3 OS Explorer OL45 The Cotswolds
•START / FINISH•	Grid reference: SP 252123
•DOG FRIENDLINESS•	Under control across farmland; on lead where requested
•PARKING•	Large car park to east of Windrush, near parish church
•PUBLIC TOILETS•	Burford High Street

BACKGROUND TO THE WALK

Often described as the gateway to the Cotswolds, the picturesque town of Burford – the oldest of the Oxfordshire medieval towns – has changed little over the years. The High Street runs down between lime trees and mellow stone houses to a narrow three-arched bridge over the River Windrush. Charles II and his mistress Nell Gwynn, whose child was named the Earl of Burford, attended Burford races and stayed at the George Hotel. When she retired to Windsor, Gwynn called her home there Burford House.

An Important Trading Centre

Situated at several major east–west and north–south crossing routes, Burford has always been regarded as an important trading centre. People would pay their tolls at the twin-gabled 15th-century Tolsey, now a museum, for the right to trade in the town and it was here that the prosperous Guild of Merchants conducted their meetings. Such was their power and influence that, by the Middle Ages, the merchants were running Burford as if it boasted a mayor and corporation.

Take a leisurely stroll through the streets of the town and you'll stumble across a host of treasures – especially in the little side-roads leading off the High Street. For example, the Great House in Witney Street was the largest residence in Burford when it was built about 1690. With its Georgian façade, it certainly dwarfs the other buildings in the street. The Dolls' House, dating back to 1939 and on view in the Tolsey Museum, is modelled on the Great House.

A Gem of a Church

Burford's parish church, with its slender spire, is one of the largest in Oxfordshire. Begun about 1170, it was enlarged over subsequent centuries and one of its last additions was the south porch, noted for its elaborate stonework. The west doorway is pure Norman, as is the central part of the tower, to which another stage was added in the 15th century to provide a base for the spire. Inside, the ceiling is fan-vaulted and there are five medieval screens dividing various chapels. In the late 1800s the church was remodelled, sparking a protest from William Morris (▶ Walk 41) and a response from the vicar that the church was his, and if he chose to he would stand on his head in it!

Levellers Revolt

The church is also associated with the Civil War Levellers – 800 Parliamentarian troopers who mutinied at Salisbury over pay, then marched north to join forces with other groups. On 14 May 1649 they reached Burford, hoping to negotiate a settlement with Fairfax, the Commander-in-Chief. However, at midnight Fairfax and Cromwell entered the town with 2,000 horsemen. Following a skirmish, they captured 340 protesters. The prisoners were held in the church, where one of them carved his name on the font. Two days later, three ringleaders were shot in the churchyard and a fourth was forced to preach a sermon.

Speaker's House

The Priory in Priory Lane is another of Burford's historic buildings. This Elizabethan house, rebuilt in the early 1800s, still has its Tudor gables and the heraldic arms over the doorway recall William Lenthall (1591–1662) who lived here and was elected Speaker to the Long Parliament in 1640.

Walk 27 Directions

① Head north along the **High Street** to the **Windrush**. Cross the river and turn right at the mini-roundabout towards Fulbrook. Pass the **Carpenters Arms** and continue along the road. Avoid a turning for Swinbrook and pass the **Masons Arms**. Keep ahead, passing **Upper End** on the left, and look for a footpath on the right by the Masons Arms sign.

② Follow the steps cut into the side of the slope up to the field edge and then swing right. Follow the boundary to a waymark just before a slope and curve left to cross the field. Go through a gap in the hedge on the far side and cross the field to an opening in the hedgerow. Cross the next field towards a curtain of woodland and make for a track.

WHERE TO EAT AND DRINK ⓘ
Burford has plenty of places to eat and drink – from hotel restaurants to pub food and tea shops. Just at the end of the walk is the **Royal Oak** which serves coffee and tea, as well as toasted teacakes. Various specials, snacks and ploughman's lunches are also available.

③ Keep right and follow the track through the woodland. Break cover from the trees and pass a row of cottages. Continue down the track to **Paynes Farm** and, just beyond it, turn right to join a signposted right of way. Head for a gate and follow the unfenced track towards trees. Descend the slope to a gate and continue ahead between hedges up the hill to the road.

④ Turn right and follow the road down into a dip. Swing left at the stone stile and sign for Widford and follow the grassy ride through verdant **Dean Bottom**. Make for a stile, turn right when you reach the T-junction and visit Widford's **St Oswald's Church**.

WHAT TO LOOK FOR ⓘ
The little medieval **Church of St Oswald**, built on the site of a Roman villa, includes a mosaic floor near the altar, discovered in 1904. Near by is the abandoned site of a medieval village; imagine the slopes of the valley crowded at one time with houses.

⑤ On leaving the church, veer right and follow the grassy track, passing a lake on the left. Turn left at the road, recross the **Windrush** and turn right at the junction. Keep to the road until you reach a footpath sign and stile on the right. Follow the riverside path across a series of stiles, eventually to reach the road. Turn right towards Burford, pass the **Great House** and the **Royal Oak** and return to the **High Street**.

WHILE YOU'RE THERE ⓘ
Visit the nearby village of **Filkins**, home to the Swinford Museum which illustrates west Oxfordshire's rural heritage. The village boasts a Victorian church built in the French Gothic style and was once the home of Sir Stafford Cripps, Chancellor of the Exchequer (1947–50) in the post-war Labour cabinet.

Abingdon's Architecture

Explore a former county town and then view it from a classic riverside path.

·DISTANCE·	7 miles (11.3km)
·MINIMUM TIME·	2hrs 45min
·ASCENT / GRADIENT·	Negligible
·LEVEL OF DIFFICULTY·	
·PATHS·	Field paths and tracks, stretches of road and Thames Path. Town and village streets (roads can be busy), 4 stiles
·LANDSCAPE·	Flat farmland and meadows south of Abingdon
·SUGGESTED MAP·	aqua3 OS Explorer 170 Abingdon, Wantage
·START / FINISH·	Grid reference: SU 503941
·DOG FRIENDLINESS·	On lead in Sutton Courtenay; not ideal in Abingdon
·PARKING·	Small car park south of the church at Sutton Courtenay
·PUBLIC TOILETS·	Various, including Old Gaol Leisure Centre and Abbey Meadow Park

BACKGROUND TO THE WALK

From a distance, driving along the nearby A34, Abingdon doesn't look much. It's all business parks and out-of-town shopping centres. But leave the car behind, stroll its ancient streets and you'll be pleasantly surprised at what you find. Until 1867 Abingdon was the county town of Berkshire, later it was swallowed up when Oxfordshire greedily expanded her borders as part of the controversial county boundary changes of 1974.

The town was originally developed around its famous abbey, founded in AD 700 and dissolved in the reign of Henry VIII. The abbey was destroyed by the Danes in the 10th century, though work began to rebuild it and William the Conqueror spent Easter here in 1084. His son Henry I appointed the Italian Abbot Foritius in 1100 and the abbey was soon acknowledged as a symbol of power and prosperity. Some of the Abbey's outbuildings still remain today, including the Gateway, over which there was a room used as a prison until the 19th century.

Often compared to Oxford's magnificent Sheldonian Theatre (▶ Walk 8), the splendid Old County Hall in the Market Place was completed in 1682 by Christopher Kempster of Burford, one of Wren's master masons during the building of St Paul's Cathedral. The Old County Hall is a perfect example of English Renaissance architecture – imposing and grand for such a small town. South of the Market Place is the Old Gaol built by Napoleonic prisoners of war between 1805 and 1811.

A Soaring Landmark

The spire of the 15th-century St Helen's Church soars above the town and can be seen for miles around. The church, which is partly 13th-century, is 108ft (33m) wide and yet only 97ft (30m) long. Inside there are five aisles, a 200-year-old candelabra and a splendid medieval painted ceiling in the Lady Chapel, representing the Tree of Jesse.

Next door to the church are the Long Alley Almshouses. These comprise Long Alley, Brick Alley and Twitty's. The oldest, Long Alley, dates from the mid-15th century. The diarist Samuel Pepys came here in 1668 and put a donation in the almsbox.

Abingdon is very much a river town, with its buildings laid out along one bank of the Thames. From the meadows on the opposite bank it is reminiscent of a seaport, with all manner of sailing craft adding a dash of colour during the summer months.

Much of Abingdon's prosperity came from cloth manufacture and the historian John Leland noted in 1549 that the town 'standeth by clothing'. In more recent years the MG car plant provided Abingdon with regular employment until its eventual closure in the 1970s.

Walk 28 Directions

① From the car park, turn left to the road, joining the adjacent tree-lined path. Take the turning for Milton and follow the road to a former pub. Turn immediately right to join a footpath. Cross a footbridge to some cottages and swing left to a kissing gate. Keep left at the immediate fork and follow

Walk 28

the path alongside the **Mill Brook**. Cross a double stile and a footbridge and continue to the next stile and footbridge.

② Turn right to join a track, following it between fields. Further on it narrows to a muddy path running between hedges. Make for the road, turn right, then bear left at the next junction, following **Drayton Road**. Take the second signposted right of way on the right.

WHILE YOU'RE THERE

Visit **Abingdon Museum**, which occupies the Old County Hall. As well as local archaeology and exhibitions, the museum houses the Southern Arts Craft Collection, which can be viewed by appointment. On the last Saturday of the month, between May and October, the balconied roof is open to the public. It was here that buns were thrown to celebrate the coronation of George III, beginning a tradition that is still upheld on royal occasions.

③ Keep ahead when the path merges with a wide track and, when it curves left by a pair of cottages, look for a stile on the right. Go diagonally across the field, briefly cutting through undergrowth into the next pasture. Keep quite close to the left boundary and aim for some tall trees and houses in the distance. Make for a footbridge in the top right-hand corner of the field. Walk ahead towards the outskirts of Abingdon and join a tarmac path. This is **Overmead**.

④ Turn right at the road and walk through the housing estate to the T-junction. Turn left and keep alongside the Thames to the **Old Anchor Inn**. Pass the pub and then turn left by some almshouses. Keep the **Church of St Helen** on the right

and head for the road. Cross over into **East St Helen Street** and make for the Old County Hall.

WHERE TO EAT AND DRINK

Abingdon has a variety of pubs from which to choose. The **Old Anchor** has a range of home-cooked food and a patio garden, while the **Broad Face** menu includes baguettes, jacket potatoes, toasties, ploughman's lunches, chicken Kiev and ham, egg and chips. The **George and Dragon** at Sutton Courtenay is a well-established village pub.

⑤ Turn right to reach **Bridge Street**, pass the **Broad Face** pub and cross the **River Thames** to the far bank. Go down the steps on the left to the tow path, pass under the road bridge and walk along the riverside path. Pass an illustrated map of Abingdon, go through a gate and cross meadows alongside the Thames, passing the ancient **Culham Bridge** on the left. Follow the line of **Culham Reach** and keep beside the water until you reach a sign for Sutton Courtenay.

⑥ Once over the cut follow the path across fields and back to the Thames. Cross several bridges and weirs at **Sutton Pools** and keep ahead at the road, passing **The Wharf** on the right. Follow the village street to the parish church and return to the car park.

WHAT TO LOOK FOR

The 12th to 14th century **church** at Sutton Courtenay is well worth a look. Herbert Asquith (1852–1928), British Liberal Prime Minister between 1908 and 1916, is buried in the churchyard, as is Eric Blair (1903–50), better known as George Orwell who, of course, wrote *Animal Farm* and *Nineteen Eighty-Four*. Blair took his pseudonym from the River Orwell in Suffolk.

A Stroll to Swift Ditch Lock

Extend the walk to a forgotten backwater of the Thames.
See map and information panel for Walk 28

•DISTANCE•	2½ miles (4km)
•MINIMUM TIME•	1hr
•ASCENT / GRADIENT•	Negligible ▲▲▲
•LEVEL OF DIFFICULTY•	👫👫 👫👫 👫👫

Walk 29 Directions
(Walk 28 option)

Having passed the **Broad Face** pub on Walk 28, make for the car park on the far side of the river (Point Ⓐ). Turn left and follow the tarmac drive towards **Rye Farm**. Pass **Kingfisher Barn** to reach some cottages and keep ahead, following the raised track across the fields. When the track eventually curves to the right, continue ahead by a line of trees. Glance back here for a good view of Abingdon church spire on the horizon. Make for a concrete bridge and keep right in the field.

Head for another bridge in the field corner and follow the path until you reach the site of the first Thames pound lock. The lock represented a significant leap forward in the way boats once travelled along the river. The remains of **Swift Ditch Lock** can just be seen in the trees. Walk alongside the lock to the point where you can see the Thames. Return to the footbridge in the field corner and go straight on along the boundary. Follow the tow path to **Abingdon Lock**, turn right and cross the weirs, where the river and the foaming water create a dramatic picture (Point Ⓑ).

On the far side of the weirs, follow the path past a wooden footbridge on the right and alongside the abbey stream for about ½ mile (800m). Cross over at the next footbridge, then turn left to walk through the abbey grounds. On the left is magnificent **Cozener's House**. Turn left into **Checker Walk** and, after a few paces, the wonderfully preserved 15th-century **Maunciper's House** is reached across a courtyard on the left. Here merchants, guests and travellers were housed by the abbey, while the maunciper, as housekeeper and almoner, saw to their needs.

In front of the Maunciper's House is the equally well-preserved Checker's or Exchequer's house, now known as the **Unicorn Theatre**. This very small, intimate theatre stages many amateur productions – everything from serious plays to restoration comedy. Inside is a chimney dating from the 13th century.

Follow the path through the arch on the far side of the courtyard and cross **Thames Street** to see the mill-wheel , which is still visible under the building of the **Upper Reaches Hotel**. Walk along Thames Street to the **Broad Face** pub, turn left, cross the bridge and rejoin Walk 28.

WALK 30

Memory Lane at Didcot

Relive the past in two museums on this delightful linear walk.

•DISTANCE•	5½ miles (8.8km)
•MINIMUM TIME•	1hr 45min
•ASCENT / GRADIENT•	Negligible
•LEVEL OF DIFFICULTY•	
•PATHS•	Urban walkway, clear field paths
•LANDSCAPE•	Town outskirts and flat farmland
•SUGGESTED MAP•	aqua3 OS Explorer 170 Abingdon, Wantage
•START / FINISH•	Grid reference: SU 525904
•DOG FRIENDLINESS•	On lead on outskirts of Didcot, in Long Wittenham and Appleford. Under control in vicinity of Bow Bridge
•PARKING•	Large car park at Didcot Parkway Station
•PUBLIC TOILETS•	Didcot Parkway Station, Pendon Museum (for visitors)

Walk 30 Directions

From the station forecourt turn left and pass **Didcot Labour Club**, then turn left at the junction 75yds (69m) beyond. Once through the railway tunnel, turn left to join a tarmac path signposted to Long Wittenham. Follow the path alongside the railway line, with the familiar chimneys of Didcot Power Station ahead of you on the horizon. Pass alongside modern housing estates, merge with another path and keep a footbridge on the left. Continue to a tunnel beneath the **A4130** and leave the outskirts of Didcot, following the path along the field edge.

Keep ahead between fence and stream and look for the outline of Wittenham Clumps (► Walk 43) on the far horizon over to the right. Make for a millennium mile post, one of 1,000 such posts to mark the creation of the National Cycle Network, and cross the road at **Bow Bridge**. Continue towards Long Wittenham, cross a bridge and

swing away from the water by a tongue of woodland. Keep on the path between fields and thick hedgerows and enter **Long Wittenham**. The tarmac path graduates to a lane before reaching **Pendon Museum** on the left.

Established on its present site in 1954, the museum reproduces, in miniature, scenes of the English countryside around 1930 – an evocative but accurate depiction of a bygone age. Exquisitely modelled cottages, farms, fields and chalky lanes recall the quiet charm of the Vale of White Horse. The museum houses many fascinating railway relics, as well as a reconstruction of a small Great Western Railway

---

WHAT TO LOOK FOR ⓘ

Didcot's huge coal-fired **power station** dominates much of this corner of Oxfordshire. The six cooling towers, built in the 1960s, are a very useful landmark for motorists and walkers. There was a great deal of opposition when they were first erected, but now they are mostly acknowledged as part of the landscape.

Walk 30

signal box. John Ahern's classic Madder Valley Railway, dating from the 1930s, is on permanent display. This fascinating relic, which pioneered scenic craftsmanship, is operated on only five days a year because of its fragile condition.

WHERE TO EAT AND DRINK ⓘ

The **Vine** and the **Plough** at Long Wittenham both serve food. Didcot has several pubs and cafés. Light refreshments are available at the **Didcot Railway Centre** and **Pendon Museum**.

Continue to the junction and war memorial and follow the main street. Pass the **Plough** and the **Vine** pubs and turn left by some thatched and timber-framed barns to reach **St Mary's Church**, cutting between two yew trees to the main door. Inside is a most impressive 12th-century font, made by casting two flat slabs of lead, embossed in the lower half with 30 figures of archbishops holding their right hands in benediction and their crosiers in their left hands. Each stands beneath a pointed arch which forms a complete arcade.

After visiting the church, return to the gate and swing right to join a footpath. Cross the churchyard to a kissing gate and follow the path as it curves left across a small pasture to reach a drive. Turn left to the road, then turn right and retrace your steps to the war memorial. Keep ahead towards the museum and turn right immediately before a cottage (No 15).

Follow the track, keeping to the left of some gates, and emerge from some trees to skirt a field, hugging the right-hand boundary. Glancing to the left reveals a good view of a railway signal, part of Pendon

Museum. Continue ahead in the field corner, cross a concrete footbridge and turn right to reach a wooden footbridge. Follow the path across the field towards trees and Appleford's church spire, just visible beyond. Make for a large oak on the far side of the field, pass into the next pasture and follow the path to the edge of Appleford. Make for the churchyard boundary, pass **Manor Farm** on the right and follow the road between houses. Keep right at the triangular junction and walk along to **Appleford Station**, from where frequent trains head back to Didcot Parkway.

When you get back, follow the signs for the **Didcot Railway Centre**, which, like the Pendon Museum, recalls the great days of steam travel. The site is operated by the Great Western Society, formed in 1961 and now one of the oldest preservation societies in Britain. The Didcot Railway Centre opened to the public in 1967, and a tour of the centre reveals the engine shed where visitors can see at first hand the magnificent collection of steam locomotives, many of them painstakingly restored over the years. A wide range of Great Western passenger coaches and a large assortment of vintage freight wagons can also be viewed.

A re-created country station is among the railway centre's many attractions, complete with its own level crossing and signal box. A unique Victorian signalling system can also be seen, as well as a faithful recreation of Brunel's broad-gauge railway. The railway centre appears regularly on television and featured prominently in a memorable *Inspector Morse* episode, *The Wolvercote Tongue*.

Thrupp's Christmas Eve Tragedy

Visit the scene of a 19th-century train crash on this gentle walk by the River Cherwell and the Oxford Canal.

•DISTANCE•	4 miles (6.4km)
•MINIMUM TIME•	1hr 45min
•ASCENT / GRADIENT•	Negligible
•LEVEL OF DIFFICULTY•	
•PATHS•	Field and waterside paths, canal tow path, 16 stiles
•LANDSCAPE•	Level countryside with Oxford Canal and River Cherwell
•SUGGESTED MAP•	aqua3 OS Explorer 180 Oxford
•START / FINISH•	Grid reference: SP 483159
•DOG FRIENDLINESS•	Under control on tow path. On lead near livestock
•PARKING•	Car park by maintenance yard at Thrupp
•PUBLIC TOILETS•	None on route

BACKGROUND TO THE WALK

Sadly, British rail disasters continue to make the newspaper headlines at the start of the 21st century. But train crashes in this country are nothing new. As you reach the railway line in the closing stages of this very pleasant waterside walk, pause for a few moments and allow the imagination to picture what happened here more than 125 years ago.

Christmas Crisis

It was 1874, about noon on Christmas Eve, and there was heavy snow on the ground. A train from London's Paddington Station, bound for the Midlands, acquired an extra coach at Oxford to help cope with the large numbers of passengers travelling home for the festivities. As the train headed north out of Oxford towards Shipton-on-Cherwell Station, a wheel-tire (tyre) on the additional coach broke. Almost at once the final carriages left the rails. The rest of the train continued for some distance before plunging down the embankment beside the Oxford Canal.

The proprietor of the nearby paper mill ran immediately to the scene of the crash. With the help of his workers and those passengers who had not sustained injury, he managed to convey the casualties to the manor house, the mill and other homes in the area. An Oxford surgeon, who had been visiting a patient at a nearby house, and a London doctor, travelling on the train, attended to the injured.

A Mission of Mercy

Some of the carriages slipped beneath the icy waters of the canal and with snow still falling and telegraph lines down, conditions that day could not have done more to hinder the rescue operation. However, word eventually reached Woodstock and Oxford and help was summoned. Even Lord Randolph Churchill, whose son Winston (▶ Walk 22) had been born just three weeks earlier, travelled over from nearby Blenheim Palace, bringing with him a supply of food and drink.

Today, we are used to the emergency services gearing swiftly into action when a disaster occurs. But in Victorian times, things moved at a much slower pace. A team of doctors eventually arrived by special train from Oxford, bringing with them vital medical supplies. Fifty of the injured passengers were taken to the Radcliffe Infirmary in the city.

Thirty passengers died in the crash, regarded then as the worst in railway history, and more than 70 were injured. Queen Victoria sent a message of sympathy. For everyone involved, Christmas was a non-event that year. The Great Western Railway set up an inquiry and an inquest was opened on Boxing Day. The jury finally ruled that what happened was an accident prompted by adverse weather conditions which affected the wheel-tire.

Several recommendations were made and there was an urgent call for more safety precautions, as well as improved testing of communication cords. Lord Randolph Churchill wrote to *The Times* demanding a more effective breaking system for all express trains.

Walk 31

Walk 31 Directions

① From the car park, pass beneath the railway line and follow the path through the plantation. Keep left at the fork and head towards the bank of the **Cherwell**. The path stays quite close to the river. Eventually you emerge from the trees into an open field. The spire of Kidlington church can be seen to the right.

Walk 31

② Draw level with the spire and look for a footbridge up ahead. Cross it to a stile and keep ahead in the field for about 50yds (46m) to a double stile and footbridge. Cross the field, aiming to the left of a bow-fronted house. Cross the next stile and go diagonally across the field to reach a stile leading out to the road.

③ Cross over to a stile, with Hampton Poyle's **St Mary the Virgin Church** seen here. Cross the pasture to the next stile, then keep to the left boundary in the field. After a few paces, look for two stiles in the hedgerow, avoid the path running extreme right and head diagonally right. Make for two gates, pass through the left one and turn immediately left across the paddock to a stile. Aim half right to the top corner of the field.

WHILE YOU'RE THERE ⓘ
Have a look at **Thrupp** and savour its colourful and bustling boating activity in the summer. Little more than a row of pretty cottages, this village used to be inhabited by those who worked on the barges, in the days when the Oxford Canal was an important route in the transportation of coal.

WHERE TO EAT AND DRINK ⓘ
The **Boat Inn** at Thrupp is a classic waterside pub. Thought to be several hundred years old, probably pre-dating the canal era, it has served several generations of boatmen and bargees down through the years. There is no food on Monday evening, but at other times expect a good range of snacks and meals. The Boat gets very busy at lunchtime and during the summer months.

④ Look for a gate here and cross a stile and footbridge a few paces from it. Go diagonally right across the field to a line of trees, pass over two wooden footbridges and head out across the next field towards a gap in the hedgerow. Cross a stile here, heading towards the ruined church at **Hampton Gay** and the remains of the manor house. Cross a stile and approach the house, veering left to the church.

⑤ Cross the railway line via a stile and make your way across the field towards trees and a footbridge over the **Cherwell**. There are two stiles here. Cross the next field towards **Shipton-on-Cherwell church** and join a track just in front of it. Make for the **Oxford Canal**, cross a stile and drop down to the tow path. Turn left and walk back to **Thrupp**.

WHAT TO LOOK FOR ⓘ
The remains of **Hampton Gay** can be seen in the fields near the Oxford Canal. In 1887, 13 years after the rail disaster, the fine 16th-century manor house here was ravaged by fire and the adjoining mill closed down. The village never really recovered and today the size of Hampton Gay is about the same as it was in medieval times. However, St Giles Church is still intact. It was built in 1767, though some sources suggest the tower dates from the 15th century.

Garsington – Agriculture and Aristocracy

Pass a delightful manor house, which became a sanctuary for some of Britain's most famous writers and artists, on this gently undulating walk.

•DISTANCE•	3 miles (4.8km)
•MINIMUM TIME•	1hr 15min
•ASCENT / GRADIENT•	165ft (50m) ▲ ▲ ▲
•LEVEL OF DIFFICULTY•	👫 👫 👫
•PATHS•	Field paths and roads (can be busy in Garsington), 11 stiles
•LANDSCAPE•	Rolling farmland to south east of Oxford
•SUGGESTED MAP•	aqua3 OS Explorer 180 Oxford
•START / FINISH•	Grid reference: SP 580024
•DOG FRIENDLINESS•	Under control where requested and on lead in churchyard
•PARKING•	Spaces near Red Lion in Garsington village
•PUBLIC TOILETS•	None on route

BACKGROUND TO THE WALK

For centuries the English village was the cornerstone of rural life. Farm labourers spent their money in the local shops and pubs and those who worked on the land or as servants in grand country houses were educated at the village school. People knew their place and didn't question it. They respected those who were seen as the pillars of the community – the landowner, the vicar and the doctor. They deferred to those above them.

The rural community is a very different place today, peopled by commuters, retired professionals and the self-employed. The class system still exists but in a very different form, and the local manor, once the domain of the local squire and a key component in the daily routine of the village, is now, in all probability, the home of a wealthy company director, a High Court Judge or a property developer.

Reminder of a Bygone Age

The manor house at Garsington is a typical example of what you might find in a traditional English village. The house is largely 16th-century and inside is an impressive staircase, various original stone fireplaces and some authentic 17th-century panelling. Near by is a 16th-century bakehouse and, beyond it, a 17th-century dovecote.

Graceful and imposing, the manor recalls a long-vanished world of style, elegance and good manners – a world inhabited by the well-heeled and the well-bred. Stand at the gate and you can picture the occupants of the house taking afternoon tea on the lawn during the summer or gathering at the front door to welcome guests as they arrived for a glittering weekend party. This would have been the scene at Garsington during the First World War and through the 1920s. At that time the manor house was the home of the noted society hostess Lady Ottoline Morrell, who died in 1938. Lady Ottoline, who was the sister of the Duke of Portland, married Philip Morrell, who represented the consituency of South Oxfordshire in Parliament and was also a member of the famous Oxford brewing family.

Walk 32

Lady Ottoline and her husband invited many of the leading literary and intellectual figures of the day to Garsington and soon it became a sanctuary for the likes of John Maynard Keynes, Virginia Woolf, T S Eliot and Bertrand Russell, among other members of the famous 'Bloomsbury Set'. Also part of this coterie were the English novelist and essayist Aldous Huxley and the poet Siegfried Sassoon. Huxley's most famous work had not yet been written when he visited Garsington. His *Brave New World*, written in 1932, is a disturbing portrayal of a Utopia peopled by human robots for whom happiness equals subordination. Sassoon used the manor as a refuge to try and rid his mind of the nightmare images provoked by his experiences as a serving soldier in the First World War.

In later years, the manor was the home of the historian Sir John Wheeler-Bennett, who witnessed the rise of Hitler's Germany when he made his home there during the 1930s. The house is not open to the public.

Walk 32 Directions

① Facing the **Red Lion**, turn left and walk through the village of **Garsington**. Veer half left at **The Hill**, leading to Sadlers Croft. Keep right and climb the bank to some bollards by the war memorial. Cross over to **The Green**, keeping the **Three Horseshoes** on the left and an historic cross on the right.

Walk 32

② Continue along the road to **St Mary's Church** and pass the **Manor House**. Keep on the road and, just as it descends quite steeply, branch left at a sign for Denton. Strike out across the field and pass between two trees. Ahead on the horizon is the hilltop church at Cuddesdon, with a curtain of trees behind it. Make for a gap in the boundary and continue in the next field. Look for a waymark in a wide gap in the next boundary and aim to the right of a copse. Pass through the gap in the field corner, avoid the path on the left and head diagonally left across the field to the far corner. Cross two stiles to reach the road.

WHILE YOU'RE THERE ℹ

Have a look at Garsington's **St Mary's Church**, which stands on high ground overlooking the surrounding countryside. Near the door is a memorial by Eric Gill, showing in relief the profile of Lady Ottoline Morrell. There are also memorials in the church to the Wickhams who lived at Garsington Manor between 1625 and 1784, farming about 350 acres (142ha).

③ Turn right and pass alongside a stone wall on the left. Walk along to the right-hand bend and bear left at the sign 'Brookside only'. Imposing **Denton House** is on the left and a striking dovecote can be seen on the right. Pass a stile and footpath on the right and keep along the lane for a few paces, turning left at a public footpath.

④ Head for a stile and pass an ornamental wall enclosing Denton House. Cross a paddock to the next stile and then go diagonally right across the field to a stile. Then head diagonally left in the next field, keeping a farm over to the right. Cross two stiles and begin

approaching the houses of Garsington. Make for a stile in the right-hand corner of the field, keeping the boundary on your right in the next pasture. Climb gently and look for a stile on the right. Cross it, turn left and make for two stiles in the field corner. Join a drive and follow it up to the road.

WHERE TO EAT AND DRINK ℹ

Garsington has a choice of pubs, among them the **Red Lion** which offers good food, cask ales and a beer garden, and the **Three Horseshoes** which has home-cooked fare and traditional beers.

⑤ Turn left towards Garsington, pass the houses of **North Manor Estate** and the village primary school before turning right, opposite **Denton Lane**, to join a footpath. Follow it to a lane, keep right and make for the road. Turn right and return to the parking area by the **Red Lion**.

WHAT TO LOOK FOR ℹ

Opposite the Three Horseshoes is a medieval **stone cross** replacing a wooden cross where services were held before the church was built. The octagonal base and stone steps are medieval but the shaft is a modern replacement. The village stocks once stood close by.

Walk 33

Watlington – a Classic Small Town

Climb into spectacular Chiltern country and enjoy views towards a famous Civil War battleground.

•DISTANCE•	5½ miles (8.8km)
•MINIMUM TIME•	2hrs
•ASCENT / GRADIENT•	200ft (60m) ▲▲ ▲ ▲
•LEVEL OF DIFFICULTY•	👣 👣 👣
•PATHS•	Field paths and tracks, stretches of road (busy), 9 stiles
•LANDSCAPE•	Level farmland and Chilterns escarpment
•SUGGESTED MAP•	aqua3 OS Explorer 171 Chiltern Hills West
•START / FINISH•	Grid reference: SU 690943
•DOG FRIENDLINESS•	On lead in Watlington; under control on Watlington Hill
•PARKING•	Town car park in Watlington
•PUBLIC TOILETS•	Watlington High Street

BACKGROUND TO THE WALK

Standing at the foot of the Chilterns escarpment, close to the Icknield Way, Watlington is one of Oxfordshire's classic old towns – small and compact, and surrounded by some of the prettiest scenery to be found in the county. During the Civil War, Watlington stood in the shadow of battle, with Royalist and Parliamentarian armies engaged in bitter conflict in the nearby fields.

Watlington's Town Hall

The quaint streets are lined with 17th-century half-timbered houses. Watlington's focal point is the gabled Town Hall, constructed in 1664. It is one of the oldest in the county. At one time a bridge connected the Town Hall to the upper floors of the nearby Hare and Hounds Hotel, now closed. The Town Hall was originally used as a a market hall, built with funds provided by one Thomas Stonor. The upper room was adapted for use as a Grammar School for boys until 1872, when a Board School was set up in premises in Davenport Place.

Another interesting building is Chiltern Gate, between the car park and Couching Street. It was opened by Lord Macclesfield in 1865 as a training school for those in domestic service. Up to 14 girls boarded here and were trained in cooking, housework and laundry. Lady Macclesfield paid some of the girls as little as six shillings per quarter.

The Missing Money Mystery

The original Hare and Hounds, which occupied a site near by, is associated with Colonel John Hampden, an MP and leader of the Parliamentary forces in the Civil War. He stayed at the inn the night before the Battle of Chalgrove Field in June 1643 and is alleged to have given the landlord, Robert Parslow, a chest containing money for the payment of troops. Hampden was fatally wounded in battle and never returned to Watlington. What happened to the chest is not known but some years later, perhaps driven by guilt, Parslow established a local charity to help the poor.

Watlington assumes the appearance of a small 18th-century market town, yet most of its streets were already complete by the 14th century. During the 1730s the existence of about 260 houses was recorded. Today many of those buildings still recall their medieval origins – narrow on the street frontage but of considerable depth, with a side passage.

Wells and Watercress

The name of the town dates back to AD 880 when it was known as Watelingtone. Springs, wells and watercress beds add to its character and the chalk used as building material in the town's early development comes from pits at the foot of the Chilterns. The people of Watlington were given certain rights – including quarrying their own chalk for building houses. By the late 17th century Nettlebed (➤ Walk 35) bricks were in use, and tiles from the same Oxfordshire village began to replace thatch.

Medieval Settlement

To find the true heart of Watlington, walk along the High Street to New Road. This, reputedly, is the centre of the original settlement. During the 13th century a manor house stood on this site and the manor court was held here. The manor house later went into decline and the king's bailiff was accused of pilfering its timber and stone. The remains of a moat can still be identified in the churchyard.

Walk 33

Walk 33 Walk 33

Walk 33 **Directions**

① Turn left out of the car park towards the town centre. Turn left at the junction, by the Town Hall, and follow **Couching Street** to the junction with **Brook Street**. Turn right and walk along to No 23. Take the footpath opposite and follow it between walls. Make for a kissing gate, keep right at the immediate fork and cross a field. Keep to the left of a tree and head for a second kissing gate. Veer left at the fork and cut between trees and fencing.

WHILE YOU'RE THERE

Watlington church, dedicated to St Leonard, is built of flint with stone dressings. Thought to date from the 12th century, the church was largely rebuilt in 1877 and includes a Victorian nave.

---

② Turn left at a track and follow it round to the right. Swing left at the 'private – no access' sign. Further on, follow the path round to the right and make for a junction with a concrete farm track. As you reach it, turn left to join a path running along the field edge. Keep the hedge and trees on the right and follow it along to a stile in the corner.

③ Turn left here and walk along the **Ridgeway** to the road. Turn right towards Nettlebed and then take the first left turning. Follow the track for about 70yds (64m) and,

when it forks at a wooden post and brick pillar, keep left and follow the enclosed path through the trees to two stiles. Continue on the path, climbing gently to a kissing gate. Keep left at the fork and keep climbing. Break cover from the trees and then enter woodland again. Go through a kissing gate and pass between beech trees to the next gate. Follow the path to the right of **Watlington Hill** car park and turn right at the road.

④ Head for **Christmas Common** and turn left at the next junction. Follow the road for about 50yds (46m) and turn left at the **Oxfordshire Way** sign. Cross a stile and keep along the field perimeter to a second stile. Keep ahead for about 70yds (64m) to a stile and leave the Oxfordshire Way at this point. Follow the sunken path, looking for white arrows on the trees, and descend gradually to a fork. Keep left alongside a chalk pit, go through a kissing gate and turn right at the road. Follow it back to the car park.

WHAT TO LOOK FOR

Given to the National Trust in 1941 by the 3rd Viscount and Viscountess Esher, **Watlington Hill** is a large area of chalk downland and copse rising to over 700ft (213m) on the north escarpment of the Chilterns. Popular with visitors and locals, the hill offers grand views and plenty of opportunity for walking.

WHERE TO EAT AND DRINK

Watlington has several pubs, including the **Carriers Arms** by the car park. Hot and cold bar snacks are available and the likes of ham, egg and chips and chicken curry feature on the menu. The **Fox and Hounds** at Christmas Common offers traditional ales and a beer garden. Imaginative and enterprising though the menu undoubtedly is, the inn is much more upmarket than it used to be so light snacks and basic meals are not very plentiful.

Christmas Common and a Civil War Truce

Climb to elegant parkland and visit a hamlet with an unusual history.
See map and information panel for Walk 33

•DISTANCE•	2½ miles (4km)
•MINIMUM TIME•	1hr 15min
•ASCENT / GRADIENT•	165t (50m) ▲▲ ▲ ▲▲
•LEVEL OF DIFFICULTY•	🚶🚶 🚶🚶 🚶

Walk 34 Directions (Walk 33 option)

From the road to Christmas Common, turn right at a footpath sign, over a stile by some galvanised gates (Point Ⓐ) and, after a few paces, you reach a gate on the right. Don't go through it, instead follow the path along the field boundary, keeping it on your right. Further down, the path runs along the edge of woodland before reaching the old farm outbuildings at **Lower Dean**. Join a track running ahead and pass a barn conversion on the left. When the track bends right, turn left through the trees to a gate, avoiding a track on the right. Make for a stile ahead and then follow the field track up the steep slope towards **Watlington Park**.

Look for a stile ahead in the trees, cross it and swing left after several paces (Point Ⓑ). On your right you can see the outline of Watlington Park. Follow the path ahead through the woods, veering right at one point. Pass a National Trust sign for **Lower Deans Wood** and continue for some time between the trees before reaching a drive.

The National Trust was founded in 1895 by three visionary Victorians whose objective was to acquire sites of historic interest and natural beauty for the benefit of the nation. The Trust's first property was the 14th-century Clergy House at Alfriston in East Sussex, purchased in 1896 for the princely sum of £10. The Trust, which is an independent charity, has come a long way since those early pioneering days.

Turn left and make for the road. Turn left, pass the little **Church of the Nativity**, built in 1889, and walk through **Christmas Common** to the **Fox and Hounds** pub.

It is said that Christmas Common takes its name from a significant day in the Civil War. By Christmas 1643, the Parliamentarians held nearby Watlington, while the Royalists defended the ridge on which Christmas Common is located. On Christmas Day itself, a temporary truce was called and both armies supposedly met on this site during the festivities – hence the name. Thus, the season of goodwill passed peacefully.

Follow the road to the junction and then rejoin Walk 33.

Wild Orchids at Warburg

Glorious scenery and a visit to a secluded nature reserve in the Chilterns.

•**DISTANCE**•	4 miles (6.4km)
•**MINIMUM TIME**•	1hr 45min
•**ASCENT / GRADIENT**•	150ft (46m) ▲▲▲
•**LEVEL OF DIFFICULTY**•	🚶 🚶🚶 🚶🚶
•**PATHS**•	Tracks, field and woodland paths, 4 stiles
•**LANDSCAPE**•	Mixture of rolling hills and wooded valleys
•**SUGGESTED MAP**•	aqua3 OS Explorer 171 Chiltern Hills West
•**START / FINISH**•	Grid reference: SU 701867
•**DOG FRIENDLINESS**•	On short lead at all times within reserve
•**PARKING**•	Room to park in vicinity of Pudding Stones
•**PUBLIC TOILETS**•	Warburg Reserve Visitor Centre

Walk 35 **Directions**

Make for the eastern end of Nettlebed **High Street** and turn left by the **Pudding Stones**. Follow the road round to the right, pass **Chapel Lane** and avoid a turning on the right. Keep left immediately beyond it at the fork, signposted 'Magpies'. Avoid a bridleway on the right and continue ahead towards **Soundess House**. The walk cuts through an avenue of trees, with glimpses here and there of glorious Chiltern country. Pass a footpath on the right and continue ahead into the trees when the track swings left at a footpath sign for Russell's Water.

Further on, merge with another track, avoiding a path on the left. Keep ahead, continue through the trees into a dry valley and soon a luxuriant curtain of trees rises up in front of you. Pass a picturesque, part timber-framed cottage on the left and turn left at the junction. Walk along to the **Warburg Reserve Visitor Centre** and car park.

The reserve, a Site of Special Scientific Interest (SSSI) is a haven of woodland and grassland, which includes a wide variety of wildlife and a nature trail. Named after an Oxford botanist, the reserve lies either side of a dry, winding valley and the pooling of cold air along the valley floor means that from time to time very hard frosts strike this delightful, though remote, corner of the county.

Covering 262 acres (106ha) and acquired in 1967, Warburg is the largest reserve managed by the Berkshire, Buckinghamshire and Oxfordshire Wildlife Trust. Its mix of partly ancient woodland, scrub and flower-rich grassland has helped to establish the site as a major visitor attraction in the area in recent years. Warburg is especially famous for its flora, with

---

WHERE TO EAT AND DRINK ⓘ

Nettlebed has the **White Hart Hotel** and the **Sun Bistro**. In nearby Highmoor is the **Dog and Duck**. If you want to stop for refreshments midway round the walk, the **Warburg Reserve** has a picnic area.

more than 450 species of plants recorded, including 15 wild orchids. Forty different kinds of butterfly have been spotted here too, as well as 450 moths and 950 fungi.

Lizards, snakes, adders, doormice, moles, hares, deer, bats and badgers are also known to inhabit the reserve. If you have the time, call into the very informative visitor centre, sit in the adjoining bird hide and watch all manner of creatures visiting the pond. You could even extend the route by following the reserve's popular Wildlife Walk.

WHAT TO LOOK FOR ⓘ

The **Pudding Stones**, at the eastern end of the village street, were formed from various deposits of boulders and flint pebbles. The precise age, origin and purpose of the stones remain a mystery, though they survive as perfect examples of some of the most ancient works of primitive peoples.

A number of trees within Warburg have been felled to create a graded interface between the grassy rides and the woodland. This produces one of the richest wildlife habitats here – attracting a wide variety of butterflies, including the dark green fritillary, the comma and the speckled wood. The felled trees leave spaces where sunlight can penetrate, with the remaining trees acting as windbreaks.

Much of the wildlife found at Warburg is struggling to survive generally throughout Britain. With increased pressure for more housing and changes in agricultural practices, the future of the countryside is under threat. Thankfully, Warburg acts as a sanctuary for wildlife – one of only a handful of sites in the country where such a rich collection of species still survives. The efforts of conservation volunteers are halting the decline of these precious plants and creatures. It is hoped that many will spread beyond the boundaries of Warburg and return to the natural habitat of the countryside.

Resuming the walk, continue ahead along the track. Eventually it parts company with the nature reserve, cutting between a line of trees and a fence. Avoid a track on the right and a stile on the left and head towards some farm outbuildings. Turn left just before the gate and go up the field slope to a stile in the trees on the right. Take the path through the woodland, climbing gently. Cross another stile and head straight across the field, looking for a stile up ahead.

Pass a pond set in the garden of a house, keep close to the left boundary and join a track. Turn left and follow it through the woodland. As the track curves right, go straight on along a path through the trees. The path veers left and climbs gently to a path. Cross over a clear path and keep ahead, following the white arrows on the tree trunks. On reaching a tree on the right with its trunk shaped like a Y, a few paces before an area of high ground drops away sharply, branch left and follow the path up to some fencing. Keep right of it and then turn right by some double gates to join a drive. Keep left at the next junction and return to the centre of **Nettlebed**.

WHILE YOU'RE THERE ⓘ

Have a look at one of Nettlebed's most famous landmarks, situated in a residential close near the village street. The village **bottle kiln**, preserved through public subscription and grants from charitable trusts, was restored in 1972.

Uffington's Galloping White Horse

Discover the legends and magic of one of Britain's greatest antiquities on this spectacular downland walk.

·DISTANCE·	7 miles (11.3km)
·MINIMUM TIME·	3hrs
·ASCENT / GRADIENT·	415ft (126m) ▲▲▲
·LEVEL OF DIFFICULTY·	🚶 🚶 🚶
·PATHS·	Ancient tracks and field paths, road (can be busy), 13 stiles
·LANDSCAPE·	Vale of White Horse and exposed downland country on Oxfordshire/Berkshire border
·SUGGESTED MAP·	aqua3 OS Explorer 170 Abingdon, Wantage
·START / FINISH·	Grid reference: SU 293865
·DOG FRIENDLINESS·	Under control or on lead in vicinity of the Uffington White Horse and along Ridgeway
·PARKING·	Large free car park near Uffington White Horse
·PUBLIC TOILETS·	None on route

BACKGROUND TO THE WALK

High above the Oxfordshire countryside stands the chalk figure of a galloping horse. Shrouded in the mists of the past, this noted 856ft (261m) high landmark, 365ft (111m) long and 130ft (40m) tall, represents one of Britain's most famous antiquities.

Mysterious and Beautiful

The best time to see the horse is early on a summer's day or during the week in the middle of winter, when the crowds and the cars are scarce. It is then that the Uffington White Horse exudes its own peculiar air of mystery. Regarded as far and away the most beautiful of all the British chalk hill figures, the horse is formed from a chalk-filled trench and, contrary to popular belief, not etched into the natural chalk. Its design is stylised, with an elegant, slender body and a distinctive beaked jaw similar to those displayed on early Iron-Age coins. There have been countless theories over the years as to its age and exact purpose.

A medieval document records it as one of the wonders of Britain, along with Stonehenge, while some sources suggest it was cut some time during the 1st century AD. Others claim it was established to celebrate King Alfred's victory over the Danes at the Battle of Ashdown in AD 871. In more recent times, the age of the horse has been scientifically pinpointed by a series of archaeological digs and analysis of soil samples, indicating that it dates back almost 3,000 years, to the late Bronze Age or early Iron Age.

Unanswered Questions

The horse is not clearly appreciated other than from the air or from some distance away – which gives credence to the theory that the White Horse may have acted as a tribal banner or badge for the inhabitants of the Vale of White Horse below. What does it symbolise and why was this particular site chosen? There are no conclusive answers. Certainly the White

Horse is closely associated with mythology. One legend claims that the figure is St George's steed and that the flat-topped chalk outcrop below, known as Dragon Hill, is where St George slew the beast. A bare patch on the summit is supposed to mark where the dragon's blood was spilt.

Literary Inspiration

The Uffington White Horse has also attracted its fair share of literary figures. G K Chesterton (1874–1936), creator of the fictional detective-priest Father Brown, wrote about it in his *Ballad of the White Horse*, and Thomas Hughes (1822–96), who was born in Uffington, described the custom of scouring the horse, clearing it of grass and weeds, in *The Scouring of the White Horse*. It was Hughes who helped revive the tradition, which at one time attracted as many as 30,000 volunteers.

Walk 36 Directions

① From the car park go through the gate and follow the outline of the grassy path along the lower slopes towards the hill. Make for a gate and cross the lane to join a bridleway. Keep left at the fork, by a bridleway waymark, and walk along to the head of Uffington's galloping **White Horse**.

② Descend steeply on the path to the tarmac access road, keeping the chalk figure on your immediate left. If you prefer to avoid the dramatic descent, retrace your steps to the lane, turn right and continue down to the junction with the **B4507**. Cross over and take the road towards Uffington, turning left at the path signposted to Woolstone. Cross the stile and keep the hedge on your right. Make for two stiles in the field corner. Continue across the next field to a stile and cut through trees to the next stile. Keep ahead with the hedgerow on your left.

WHERE TO EAT AND DRINK

The **White Horse Inn** at Woolstone is directly on the route of the walk and serves food. Alternatively, try the **Blowing Stone** at nearby Kingston Lisle which offers an extensive menu and a pleasant conservatory restaurant.

---

③ Cross the stile, turn left at the road and walk through the village of **Woolstone**. Turn left by the **White Horse Inn** and follow the road to **All Saints Church**. As you approach it, veer right across the churchyard to a stile and gate. Cross a paddock to a further gate and stile. Turn left up the road and turn right at the footpath sign. Follow the edge of the field, keeping the hedge on your left-hand side, eventually reaching a stile. Turn right and walk through the trees to a footbridge. Cross the footbridge to a field, head diagonally left to a stile and turn right. Follow the field

edge to a stile within sight of a thatched cottage. Cross it and go ahead to another stile leading out to a road. The cottage is now level with you on the left.

④ Cross the road and follow the D'Arcy Dalton Way, signposted on the opposite side. Make for a stile, cross a paddock and head for the road by the village sign for **Compton Beauchamp**. Cross over and take the drive to the church, next to the manor. Retrace your steps to the sign and walk up to meet the junction with the **B4507**. Cross over and climb quite steeply to the **Ridgeway**.

⑤ Turn right if you wish to visit **Wayland's Smithy** (➤ While You're There). Otherwise, turn left to continue the walk. Follow the track to a crossroads signed 'Woolstone' and continue on the Ridgeway uphill to reach the grassy ramparts of **Uffington Castle** on your left. Leave the track here, cut through the remains of the fort to the access road and return to the car park at the start of the walk.

WHAT TO LOOK FOR

All Saints Church at Woolstone is a lovely chalk-built church. Inside you'll find a lead font and some striking 20th-century Stations of the Cross. During the Second World War, a German bomb blew out all the windows. Close by is the tiny village of **Compton Beauchamp**, with its Tudor and Georgian manor house (not open to the public).

WHILE YOU'RE THERE

Visit **Wayland's Smithy**, just off the route. This impressive 5,000-year-old long barrow occupies a remote, ghostly setting seemingly miles from civilisation. According to legend, Wayland's Smithy got its name from the Norse god, Wayland the Smith, who made shoes for the White Horse. Crowning Whitehorse Hill is **Uffington Castle**, an Iron-Age hill fort situated high on the Ridgeway, Britain's oldest road. The hill fort covers about 8 acres (3ha) and is enclosed by a rampart and a deep outer ditch.

Stonor Park and a Secret Printing Press

Explore the rolling countryside of the Chiltern Hills before crossing a beautiful deer park.

•DISTANCE•	3½ miles (5.7km)
•MINIMUM TIME•	1hr 15min
•ASCENT / GRADIENT•	150ft (46m) ▲▲▲
•LEVEL OF DIFFICULTY•	林 林 林
•PATHS•	Wood and parkland paths and tracks, country lanes, 2 stiles
•LANDSCAPE•	Spectacular Chilterns
•SUGGESTED MAP•	aqua3 OS Explorer 171 Chiltern Hills West
•START / FINISH•	Grid reference: SU 735883
•DOG FRIENDLINESS•	On lead where signs request it, especially in Stonor Park
•PARKING•	Off-road at southern end of Stonor, by barns of Upper Assendon Farm, which straddle road
•PUBLIC TOILETS•	Stonor Park, for visitors; otherwise none on route

BACKGROUND TO THE WALK

Without question, the chief attraction of this walk is Stonor House, set in its own magnificent parkland amid the rolling Chilterns and open to the public at various times of the year. There has been a house here since the Norman Conquest – the core of the present one dates from the medieval period and has been enlarged and restored a great many times over the years.

The 18th-century façade of red brick encloses an E-shaped Elizabethan house with work dating from an earlier era behind it. Within its walls lies a maze of rooms and staircases, with sculptures, tapestries, drawings, paintings and many items of fine furniture on display.

Campion the Martyr

Stonor is also known for its 14th-century Chapel of the Holy Trinity, and it was here in 1580 that Lady Stonor gave refuge to the Jesuit priest and martyr Edmund Campion. Born in London in 1540, Campion was educated at Christ's Hospital in Sussex and St John's College, Oxford. He later became a deacon in the Church of England but fled to Douai in France when his Roman Catholic leanings became apparent. In 1573 he joined the Society of Jesus in Bohemia.

Campion became Professor of Rhetoric at Prague but returned to England in 1580 for a Jesuit mission. He preached in this part of the Chilterns and lived in secret at Stonor House, which at that time was a refuge for Catholics. The Stonor family was of the same faith and as a direct result of their religious devotion, endured persecution and imprisonment as well as the loss of many of their estates during the 16th and 17th centuries.

Here, using a printing press in a hidden room of the house, Campion supervised the printing of his book *Decem Rationes* (The ten reasons [for being a Catholic]), distributing 400 copies in St Mary's, Oxford, before the degree-giving ceremony in June 1581.

Trial and Execution

As a consequence of what he did, Campion was arrested, while preaching at Lyford in Berkshire, by a spy, George Eliot. He was tried on a charge of conspiracy and, having refused to renounce his faith, executed on 1 December. Before he was hanged, he wrote: 'If our religion do make us traitors we are worthy to be condemned, but otherwise we are and have been good subjects as ever the queen had.' Campion was beatified in 1886 and later canonised as one of the 40 Martyrs of England and Wales. His feast day is 25 October.

A visit to Stonor House is certainly memorable, but a stroll through its glorious deer park and beechwoods makes a lasting impact – particularly on a bright day in late October when the leaves are beginning to turn and the autumn sun bathes the surroundings in a glorious golden light.

Walk 37 Directions

① Make for the 30mph speed restriction sign at the southern end of **Stonor** and turn left at the stile just beyond it to join a footpath.

Keep the farm outbuildings on your left and go up the slope towards trees. Cross a stile into the woodland and begin climbing very steeply into the Chilterns. Look for the white arrows on tree trunks and further up you reach a clear

Walk 37

WHILE YOU'RE THERE ⓘ
There's plenty to see inside **Stonor** house. Have a look at the dining-room wallpaper which depicts panoramic views of the buildings of Paris. Even more memorable than that, perhaps, are the luxurious bed and chairs shaped like open scallops to be found in the bedroom of Francis Stonor.

track on a bend. Continue ahead, cross a track and pass alongside **Coxlease Farm**.

② Keep to the right of the outbuildings and join a track leading to the farmhouse. Make for the road and turn left. Pass several properties and follow the lane between hedges. Avoid a path on the right and, further on, the path bends sharp right. Ignore the bridleway on the left for Stonor and keep on the road which curves left and runs alongside **Kildridge Wood**, an area of mixed woodland and bracken. Pass some double wooden gates on the right and keep to the road as it curves right. Turn left after a few paces, signposted towards Southend.

WHERE TO EAT AND DRINK ⓘ
The **Stonor Arms** in the village of Stonor has an award-winning restaurant and stylish accommodation. If you're looking for something more modest, try Blades, an informal bar situated within the building and decorated with fascinating rowing memorabilia. **Stonor Park** has a tea room.

③ Keep Kildridge Wood on the left still, with views over fields and rolling countryside on the right. Follow the lane until you reach a turning on the left – the **Chiltern Way**. Follow the path beside a pair of brick and flint cottages, following the way towards **Stonor Park**. Cross

a junction of tracks and descend between trees. Some of the trunks carry the CW symbol for Chiltern Way. Keep left at the fork, passing between laurel bushes and trees, and eventually you reach a deer fence and gate.

④ Pass alongside a tall wire fence and gradually the view of **Stonor** house edges into view. Head down towards the road and look for a kissing gate in the deer fence. Turn left and head for **Stonor** village. Pass a footpath and a turning to **Maidensgrove** and keep ahead to the **Stonor Arms**. Continue through the village and return to the parking area.

WHAT TO LOOK FOR ⓘ
Stonor is a good base for exploring the **Chilterns**. These rolling hills, many of them covered with glorious beechwoods, stretch for miles, and on some paths or tracks within the region you may catch sight of red kites, which have been reintroduced to the area.

Walk 38

Wallingford and William the Conqueror's Castle

Discover the ancient treasures of a famous town on the Thames before following a pretty stretch of riverbank.

•DISTANCE•	3 miles (4.8km)
•MINIMUM TIME•	1hr 30min
•ASCENT / GRADIENT•	Negligible
•LEVEL OF DIFFICULTY•	
•PATHS•	Bridleways, pavements, Thames Path, 11 stiles
•LANDSCAPE•	Flat farmland by Thames
•SUGGESTED MAP•	aqua3 OS Explorer 70 Abingdon, Wantage
•START / FINISH•	Grid reference: SU 604895
•DOG FRIENDLINESS•	Mostly on lead or under strict control; on short lead at nature reserve
•PARKING•	Long-stay car park in St George's Road, Wallingford
•PUBLIC TOILETS•	Off High Street in Wallingford

BACKGROUND TO THE WALK

Wallingford is one of those towns that can hold your attention for hours. Its churches are well worth a look, its museum and Town Hall attract many visitors, and the grass-covered mounds of its ruined castle serve as a reminder of the bitter struggle for supremacy during the Civil War. Wallingford has even made guest appearances in television drama – most recently as the town of Cawston in the popular thriller series *Midsomer Murders*. Scenes were filmed in the Market Place.

My first proper visit to Wallingford was early on a Sunday evening in late March. Church bells were summoning parishioners to evensong, the streets were pleasantly quiet and there was a hint of spring in the air. This little riverside town remains one of my favourite places in the county.

A Royalist Stronghold

Turning the pages of history, you'll find Wallingford was once acknowledged as an important river crossing, and in the 11th century William the Conqueror deemed a large castle was necessary to protect it. William crossed the Thames here in 1066 and today the river is spanned by a splendid 900-ft (274m) bridge of 16 arches. The castle was the last Royalist stronghold in Oxfordshire to surrender, following a brave Parliamentary siege that lasted 65 days. Cromwell ordered it to be demolished six years later.

Elsewhere, there is much to see. The Town Hall is one of Wallingford's finest buildings. Resting on pillars, it houses the tourist information centre. Inside the Town Hall are portraits by Lawrence and Gainsborough, as well as a silver mace and the 15th-century town seal. In front of the building is a striking war memorial, unveiled in 1921.

Across the road is the 19th-century Corn Exchange, now a theatre. Look for the Victorian drinking fountain at the northern end of the Market Place, given to Wallingford by Alderman Hawkins, who ran a draper's shop in the town.

Wallingford's Wonderful Churches

No visit to Wallingford is complete without a look at its churches (the town once had 16, but there are now only six). One of the most striking of these holy buildings is St Peter's Church with its needle-like spire. The church, which was rebuilt in 1769–77, contains the tomb of Sir William Blackstone (1723–80), Oxford's first professor of English law, who presented St Peter's with a clock from Horse Guards in London.

Not far away, along Thames Street, and defining the south east corner of the old Saxon walled town, is St Leonard's Church. The churchyard, which has been managed by a wildlife conservation group since 1996, is a haven for wildlife in an urban setting. To facilitate improved conservation, the churchyard has been divided into various areas, each with its own distinct environmental features. It's worth allowing time to stroll through the churchyard, which you pass towards the end of the walk, as it reveals a variety of habitats and wildlife surprises.

Walk 38

Walk 38 Directions

① On leaving the car park turn left and walk along **St George's Road**. Turn left into **High Street** and head towards Wallingford town centre. Pass the library and **Wallingford Museum** and keep ahead to the junction with **St Martin's Street** and **Castle Street**. The Town Hall is on the right and the remains of the castle on the left. Continue over the junction and pass **Lamb Arcade** and the **George Hotel**. On the right is the spire of St Peter's Church in Thames Street.

> **WHERE TO EAT AND DRINK** ⓘ
> Wallingford has a choice of pubs, hotels and tea rooms from which to choose. There's the **George Hotel** and the **Town Arms** directly on the route, while further afield, at Cholsey, is the **Morning Star**, offering basic meals and snacks.

② Pass the **Town Arms** and cross the bridge over the Thames. Continue along the road and, about 80yds (73m) beyond the traffic-lights, turn right at a bridleway signposted 'Ridgeway and Grim's Ditch'. Follow the enclosed track between fences, keeping the river and adjacent meadows to your right. Keep left at a waymark and stay on the bridleway. Cross a footpath and now the woodland gives way to open fields.

③ On reaching a junction with a concrete farm track, turn right and head towards the buildings of **Newnham Farm**. Keep left and walk along the track to **St Mary's Church** at Newnham Murren. With the church on your right, continue on the tree-lined bridleway. Approaching the **A4130**, veer right at the 'cyclists dismount' sign and follow the pavement along to a bridge over the **Thames**. Once over the bridge, veer right and follow the tarmac path down the bank to the riverside.

> **WHILE YOU'RE THERE** ⓘ
> **Wallingford Museum** is housed in part of a medieval hall-house. One of its major attractions is a time-warp walk through Saxon and medieval Wallingford with personal audio commentary. Also on display are a Victorian shop, a pub and a model of Wallingford Station.

④ Turn left and head upstream towards Wallingford, passing a boathouse. Continue on the Thames Path to a tarmac drive running between houses. Just beyond a property called **The Boathouse**, turn right by a flood marker, dated 1894. Follow the path to the road by **St Leonard's Church**. Turn right and follow the road along to **St Peter's Street**. Turn left here, then left again into **Wood Street**. After 70yds (64m) turn right into **Mousey Lane** and make for the Town Hall. Retrace your steps along **High Street** to reach the car park at the start of the walk.

> **WHAT TO LOOK FOR** ⓘ
> As you cross the River Thames at Wallingford, in the early stages of the walk, look down to your left and you'll spot a **memorial stone** which recalls that the field here was presented to the borough by Alderman and Mrs Lester in memory of their son, who was killed in action in 1944, aged 27.

Cholsey's Crime Queen

Visit the grave of a famous author on this pleasant spur to Cholsey.
See map and information panel for Walk 38

•DISTANCE•	9 miles (14.5km)
•MINIMUM TIME•	3hrs 30min
•ASCENT / GRADIENT•	Negligible
•LEVEL OF DIFFICULTY•	

Walk 39 Directions
(Walk 38 option)

Turn right and follow the Thames Path under the **A4130** road bridge (Point Ⓐ). Keep along the tow path, passing the buildings of **Carmel College** on the opposite bank. Go through a series of galvanised gates and **Brookes University boathouse** on the right. Cross fields and meadows and gradually the Fair Mile Hospital buildings edge into view. Enter **Cholsey Marsh Nature Reserve** and pass a seat by the river.

Turn right as the Thames Path leaves the riverbank (Point Ⓑ). The track graduates to a lane before reaching the **A329**. Cross over into **Papist Way** and pass the **Morning Star** on the left. Continue through Cholsey and cross **Station Road** into **West End**. Avoid the railway bridge and bridleway as the road curves right and head for **Sandy Lane** (Point Ⓒ).

Turn left opposite it on an enclosed footpath, avoiding a footbridge on the right. Pass beneath the Cholsey and Wallingford railway and turn immediately right at a bridge over a stream. Walk alongside the railway to a footbridge and kissing gate.

Skirt the next field, heading towards the church. Make for the field corner where there is a footbridge and gate. Cross the field to the churchyard (Point Ⓓ). To visit Agatha Christie's grave and its imposing headstone, keep to the left of the church and it will be found along the back wall.

Agatha Christie (1890–1976) lived at nearby Winterbrook House, having previously lived at Sunningdale in Berkshire. A prolific crime writer, she is probably best remembered for her play *The Mousetrap* – a classic whodunit – which celebrated 50 years on the London stage in November 2002, and shows no sign of closing.

Make for the churchyard exit and cross the road to a stile. Go diagonally right across the field to a stile by the railway. Follow the line for some time, crossing eight stiles to reach a track crossing the railway. Veer right here and walk along to the **A4130**. Cross it to a stile and follow a grassy path between fields. Approach **Winterbrook** and turn left when you get to the road. Pass **Winterbrook House** on the right and walk along to a sign for the Thames Path National Trail. Follow the path beside a tributary stream of the Thames and rejoin Walk 38 at the riverbank.

Old Father Thames at Goring

Follow the tow path beside the Thames and return to the start by train.

•DISTANCE•	5½ miles (8.8km)
•MINIMUM TIME•	2hrs
•ASCENT / GRADIENT•	90ft (25m) ▲ ▲ ▲
•LEVEL OF DIFFICULTY•	栋 栋 栋
•PATHS•	Tow path, field and woodland paths, village roads, no stiles
•LANDSCAPE•	Thames Valley meadows and beechwoods
•SUGGESTED MAP•	aqua3 OS Explorer 171 Chiltern Hills West
•START / FINISH•	Grid reference: SU 602805
•DOG FRIENDLINESS•	Under control on Thames Path; on lead in villages
•PARKING•	Station car park or public car park off Station Road in Goring
•PUBLIC TOILETS•	Station Road car park and Pangbourne main car park

Walk 40 Directions

From the station follow the road signposted 'village centre', and go down the **High Street**, passing the **Miller of Mansfield** pub and the village hall, dated 1925. Look for the Thames Path sign and join the tow path.

The end of Ferry Lane, over on the left, represents the point where the Ridgeway and the Icknield Way once crossed the river at a ford. Both paths originally formed a prehistoric trade route between Dorset and East Anglia. The ford was important to the Romans and resulted in a raised causeway here. Settlements were established by the crossing and in Anglo-Saxon times the river became a vital frontier. Streatley, over on the Berkshire bank, was part of Wessex, while Goring was in Mercia.

Head downstream with the river on your right. Follow the trail, passing some seats and a little grassy clearing before reaching a boathouse. Beyond it the path skirts meadows and fields, on its way to Gatehampton. There used to be a ferry here, one of many services along the entire length of the Thames, but most of them were discontinued during the Second World War.

> **WHERE TO EAT AND DRINK**
> The **Queen's Arms** by Goring railway station serves a range of traditional meals and snacks. Alternatively, try the **Miller of Mansfield** near the Thames in Goring, or the **Cross Keys** in Pangbourne.

The Thames is historically the most important river in Britain, used as a highway since early times. To stroll along its banks is the only way to appreciate its unique beauty and character. The 180-mile (290km) Thames Path, officially opened in July 1996 by the Countryside Commission (now the Countryside Agency), is the only long distance national trail in the country to follow a river for its entire length. Over 13 million people live within its catchment area and with numerous access points, frequent

Walk 40

public transport services, a high standard of waymarking and many points of interest, the Countryside Agency believes its long-term popularity is assured.

The user-friendly terrain and level, easy-going surface enable walkers to tackle the route at any time of year, though stretches of the riverbank can become wet and muddy after prolonged rain. More than 95 per cent of the trail currently follows the intended route, running beside the river, which begins life as a trickling stream in a Gloucestershire field near Cirencester.

Despite problems over prohibited access in several places, the Thames Path has come a long way since the 1920s when the concept of providing public access along the length of the river was first mooted. Over the years, increasing public demand for recreation and access to the countryside led to the eventual designation of the route in 1989. Much of the Thames Path is set against an urban background but, even here, there are many distinguished buildings and famous monuments to be seen, reflecting Britain's history and tradition.

The rural stretches are plentiful, too, and will satisfy those who seek peace and solitude. The Thames Path, which frequently changes from one bank to the other and in London follows both banks simultaneously, can easily be completed in stages or as a two-week walking holiday.

Between Wallingford and Reading, the Thames is most closely associated with the 'Goring Gap' where, during the ice age, the river carved a new passage through the chalk hills, cutting between the Berkshire Downs and the Chilterns.

Pass a pill box, a reminder of the dark days of 1940 when Britain faced a very real threat of invasion, and follow the trail beneath Brunel's original Paddington-to-Bristol railway line. Pass through several galvanised gates and walk along to a gate for **Ferry Cottage**. At this point turn left, away from the riverbank. On reaching a T-junction, turn right and follow the path parallel to the Thames, cutting between the trees of **Hartslock Wood**. Look for another pill box down to your right, partly concealed by woodland, and keep ahead. The river is glimpsed between the trees as you climb steadily above it.

Emerge at length from the woodland and continue between fields. Climb a flight of steep steps and keep ahead on a drive, passing **Elm Cottage** and **Coombe Park Farm**. Turn right at the road, pass several properties – the **White House** and **Milverton** – then follow the road round and down into **Whitchurch** village. Pass **Manor Road**, the **Greyhound** pub and the **Ferryboat Inn** before reaching the toll bridge.

Cross the Thames to the **Adventure Dolphin Centre** at Pangbourne on the Berkshire bank, then turn right by the Boathouse surgery and follow the waymarked footpath to the road. Opposite is **Pangbourne railway station** where you catch the train back to Goring.

WHAT TO LOOK FOR

Whitchurch Bridge is a Victorian toll bridge distinguished by its white lattice architecture. Motorists pay to cross the bridge but pedestrians go free. The bridge is privately owned.

Buscot to Kelmscott

On the Thames Path to the home of William Morris.

•DISTANCE•	4¾ miles (7.7km)
•MINIMUM TIME•	2hrs
•ASCENT / GRADIENT•	82ft (25m) ▲ ▲ ▲
•LEVEL OF DIFFICULTY•	🚶 🚶 🚶
•PATHS•	Riverside paths, fields, village lanes, 7 stiles
•LANDSCAPE•	Open, flat lands of the Thames floodplain
•SUGGESTED MAP•	aqua3 OS Explorer 170 Abingdon, Wantage
•START / FINISH•	Grid reference: SU 231976
•DOG FRIENDLINESS•	Lead required around weir, not permitted in Manor gardens
•PARKING•	National Trust car park (free) in Buscot, signed 'Buscot Weir'
•PUBLIC TOILETS•	Buscot, behind phone box

BACKGROUND TO THE WALK

The village of Kelmscott is famous for its connections with the founder of the Arts and Crafts Movement, William Morris (1834–96). Although he was also a talented poet and a pioneering socialist, today he is best remembered for his furnishing designs, rich with flowers, leaves and birds, still popular on fabric and wallpaper.

Champion of Fine Craftsmanship

Throughout his life, working with the great Pre-Raphaelite artists such as Edward Burne-Jones and Dante Gabriel Rossetti, Morris dedicated himself to a movement against what he saw as the vulgar tastes of his day, with its sentimentality, clutter and gaudy gewgaws. He put a new value on craftsmanship, studying and experimenting with the techniques of ages past, and so developing a style of apparent simplicity combined with functionality. He took it upon himself to educate as well as create, with pronouncements such as – 'Have nothing in your houses that you do not know to be useful, or believe to be beautiful' – emphasising the place of good design in everyday life. His philosophy of design became hugely influential and is still popular today.

Morris looked to the medieval artists and architects for his inspiration – a favourite outing for visitors to Kelmscott was to the magnificent Great Barn, a medieval stone-built tithe barn at nearby Great Coxwell (now cared for by the National Trust), to admire the intricacies and craftsmanship of its soaring timber roof.

Manor and Village

Kelmscott Manor itself dates from 1570 and became Morris's country home in 1871. It's a mellow old place, built of the local grey limestone, with mullioned windows and high pointed gables topped by ball finials. (The image is familiar from the woodcut designed for the Kelmscott Press, which he founded in 1890.) Morris loved the manor for its integrity and austerity, and for the harmony of the house in its setting, almost as if 'it had grown up out of the soil.' Now owned by the Society of Antiquaries of London, the house is open to the public on Wednesdays and some Saturdays through the summer, and contains many examples of Morris's work.

William Morris's influence on the area continued even after his death. As a memorial to the great man, several structures were designed to his principles and built in Kelmscott village, notably Memorial Cottages and next-door Manor Cottages. Reflecting traditional style but with a modern, practical twist, they blend effortlessly into the village and were overseen by his widow Jane and daughter May (herself an accomplished designer). On a wider scale, Morris's work did much for the emergence of a Cotswold identity in the 1920s, with his appreciation and publicising of the vernacular architecture.

Morris is buried with his wife and daughters in the churchyard at Kelmscott, under a modest tombstone, its only adornment the elegant lettering designed by Philip Webb.

Walk 41

Walk 41 Directions

① Turn left and walk back into **Buscot** to admire the arcaded pump. Retrace your steps and continue ahead on the road, signed to the weir. The road becomes a track. Follow it round the edge of

the **Village Field** and cross a bridge. Keep right, to pass **Lock Cottage**. Follow the footpath over the weir. Bear left and cross the lock gate.

② Turn right, cross a stile and follow the path beside the river. Soon bear left and cross a bridge, with a view left to the main weir.

Walk 41

Turn right and follow the **Thames Path** beside the meandering river. Cross a stile, and continue past two wartime pill boxes and a gate. Go through a pair of gates. The roofs of Kelmscott appear ahead. Go through a gateway and continue towards the bridge, passing through some trees.

③ Pass the bridge, go through a gate and turn left up the field. At the far side cross a stile and two footbridges. Bear left and ahead up the hedge (yellow waymarker). At the end turn right along the path, which may be overgrown. Follow this into **Kelmscott** village.

> **WHAT TO LOOK FOR** ⓘ
> Look out for the charming relief carving of William Morris, set in the wall of the pair of **Memorial Cottages** at first-floor height, between the windows. The great man is shown sitting under a tree, listening to the birds, with the old wool barn and summer house of the manor in the background.

④ Turn right to pass the **Plough Inn**. Bear left along the road, passing **Memorial Cottages** and **Manor Cottages**. Keep right to reach **Kelmscott Manor**. Maintain your direction ahead down the track, pass a Second World War pill box, and turn right just before you get to the river.

⑤ Cross a bridge and go through a gate to join the **Thames Path National Trail**. Cross a stile and

> **WHERE TO EAT AND DRINK** ⓘ
> The friendly **Plough Inn** at Kelmscott is a lovely old pub, with a flagstone floor and beautifully refurbished oak panelling. There's a beer garden at the front and a restaurant at the rear, with a lunch menu that changes according to the season – from mushrooms on toast to more exotic pasta dishes, as well as sandwiches. Dogs are welcome at the bar. **Buscot Village Shop** doubles as a tea room, also serving light lunches. Both are closed on Mondays.

continue, passing another old wartime pill box on your left. Go through the gate by the footbridge and turn left over the bridge. Bear left and right over another bridge. Cross a stile and walk up the track. Soon this crosses a ditch; now head diagonally right across the field. At the corner cross a stile and footbridge by the fingerpost and turn right. Keep straight on up the edge of the field, with views of Buscot House, left. Follow the track downhill, and bend right, then turn left over a footbridge. Continue on the path diagonally right across the next two fields.

⑥ Go through a gate by the road and turn right up a drive. Look out for a yellow waymarker and take the footpath off to the left. Soon cross a stile and veer left along the edge of the field. Cross a stile and a footbridge at the other end, walk across the **Village Field** and turn left to retrace your route back to the start of the walk in **Buscot**.

> **WHILE YOU'RE THERE**
> **St Mary's Church** at Buscot has some good examples of stained glass from the firm of Morris and Co, founded by William Morris in 1861. The colours are rich, the foliage sumptuous in its detail and the angels elegantly Pre-Raphaelite. The window above the altar is by Burne-Jones. Look, too, for the unusual painted pulpit and two touching marble memorials to the first and second wives of Edward Loveden Loveden Esq, who died within four years of each other.

Mysteries at Minster Lovell

A gentle stroll through meadows and woods beside the Windrush.

•DISTANCE•	4 miles (6.4km)
•MINIMUM TIME•	1hr 30min
•ASCENT / GRADIENT•	180ft (55m)
•LEVEL OF DIFFICULTY•	
•PATHS•	Meadows, tracks, pavement and lane, woodland, 17 stiles
•LANDSCAPE•	Shallow, fertile valley of River Windrush
•SUGGESTED MAP•	aqua3 OS Explorer 180 Oxford
•START / FINISH•	Grid reference: SP 321114
•DOG FRIENDLINESS•	Lead essential on road through Crawley and Minster Lovell
•PARKING•	Car park (free) at eastern end of Minster Lovell, above church and hall
•PUBLIC TOILETS•	None on route

BACKGROUND TO THE WALK

Crawley's industrial heart is announced by its tall mill chimney, which dominates the shallow, verdant valley to the north of Witney. By comparison, just a mile or two to the west, old Minster Lovell is the very essence of an idealised Cotswold village. Its little houses of grey-brown stone straggle up a narrow village street, adorned with impossibly pretty cottage gardens. At the top is a golden stone church, looking down over a silvery meander of the River Windrush. At the bottom is a charming old pub, the Swan, with the former mill opposite tastefully restored and now part of a discreet conference centre.

Two villages appeared on the site in the Domesday survey – Minster Lovell and Little Minster, separated by the river. There's now a newer Minster Lovell to the south west, an experimental housing and allotment development dating back to the 1840s. However, it's the picturesque older settlement which engages visitors.

No perfect Cotswold village would be complete without its manor house, of course. And Minster Lovell's is a beauty, although in ruins. The site, in a curve of the river below the church, was picked out by Lord William Lovell, 7th Baron of Tichmarsh, in the 1440s. William's son John extended the new manor house, and signboards among the broken walls show how splendid it must have been, complete with a massive gatehouse.

A Gruesome Tale

William's grandson, Francis, was politically the most successful member of the family, but came to a nasty end. Raised as a Yorkist, he served as Lord Chamberlain to Richard III and fought with him at Bosworth Field in 1485. The King died in the battle and Francis took refuge in Flanders. Two years later he returned to take part in the Lambert Simnel rebellion, which backed an Oxford baker's boy for the throne.

On the losing side in a battle at Stoke in 1487, Lovell fled home and was never heard of again. However it is said that in 1708, while a new chimney was being built at Minster Lovell Hall, a locked vault was discovered. In it was the skeleton of the missing Viscount Lovell, sitting with his papers at a table. Suddenly exposed to the air, the corpse dissolved into a cloud of dust in an instant. It was assumed that he had hidden here with the help of a servant, who subsequently fell ill and died, leaving unknown the secret of his master's whereabouts. John Buchan made memorable and chilling use of the legend in his novel *The Blanket of the Dark* (1931).

A pioneer of modernised agricultural techniques, Thomas Coke was the last resident at the Hall. He left in 1747 for his new Norfolk home, Holkham Hall. The old house was dismantled and the ruins are now cared for by English Heritage.

Walk 42 Directions

① Walk up the lane, signposted 'Crawley'. At the end of the village cross a stile, right, and take the footpath diagonally left across the field, also signposted 'Crawley'. Look right for a view of the ruins of **Minster Lovell Hall** and the circular dovecote. Cross a stile and continue straight on along the path, with a

Walk 42

stone wall to your left. The mill chimney ahead on the horizon belongs to Crawley Mill.

② Cross a stile and go ahead up a slight incline. Cross another stile, go through a gate and continue on the path, walking up a green tunnel of a lane. Pass above **Crawley Mill**. At the road turn right and follow this down into **Crawley**. At the bottom look left to admire the diminutive village green with its stone cross. The **Lamb Inn** is on the left.

③ Turn right and follow the pavement past **Manor Farm**, with its huge pond. Cross the humpback bridge over the **Windrush** – look right for a good view of the old mill house. At the other side of the bridge cross the road and turn left through a gate, signed 'Witney'. Follow the bridleway beside the stream, marked by a line of willows.

④ At the junction of paths by a gate look ahead and left to see **New Mill**. Turn right through the gate and walk up the field edge. Pass a gate and cross the road. Climb the stile, go straight on to a second stile, and follow the path down through the woods.

⑤ At the bottom cross a stile and follow the path along the fence. The wildflower meadows of **Maggots Grove** lie to your right. Continue over three more stiles and bear left beside the trees. Cross a stile by a meander of the river.

⑥ Cross a further stile and enter the woods. At a gate bear right, following the arrows, and cross two footbridges. After a short distance cross a bridge over the river. Go through a squeeze gate towards **Minster Lovell Hall**. Climb the stile and go through a gate to explore the ruins.

⑦ Leave by the top entrance and walk through the churchyard. Cross a slab stile, continue along a grassy path with the village up to your right. Cross a footbridge and stile and veer to the right. Cross one stile and then another into **Wash Meadow** recreation ground. Keep right and go through a gate on to the high street, with the **Old Swan Inn** to your left. Turn right and walk up through the village to the car park at the start of the walk.

Dorchester – from Cathedral City to Commuter Village

Soak up the atmosphere of an ancient settlement before climbing to an outstanding viewpoint above the Thames.

•DISTANCE•	4½ miles (7.2km)
•MINIMUM TIME•	1hr 45min
•ASCENT / GRADIENT•	115ft (35m) ▲ ▲ ▲
•LEVEL OF DIFFICULTY•	🚶🚶 🚶🚶 🚶🚶
•PATHS•	Field and woodland paths and tracks, stretch of Thames Path and main road with pavement
•LANDSCAPE•	Thames Valley
•SUGGESTED MAP•	aqua3 OS Explorer 170 Abingdon, Wantage
•START / FINISH•	Grid reference: SU 578939
•DOG FRIENDLINESS•	Under control in vicinity of Day's Lock and at Little Wittenham Nature Reserve. On lead near livestock
•PARKING•	Parking area in Bridge End at southern end of Dorchester
•PUBLIC TOILETS•	At parking area

BACKGROUND TO THE WALK

Dorchester is steeped in history. On the surface it seems to represent the quintessential English village, inhabited by commuters and retired professionals. But there is much more to it than quaint winding streets and rows of chocolate-box cottages. The Romans built an important town here, Dorocina, though its ramparts are now only faintly recognisable, and the present abbey stands on the site of the first Saxon cathedral in Wessex.

Excavations have revealed a number of Roman artefacts in the locality – among them an altar to Jupiter and Augustus, various tessellated pavements and some Roman coins. Who knows what other relics of their occupation may lie beneath surface.

A Very Special Abbey

In effect, Dorchester is one of our oldest cities, though it seems hard to believe looking at it today. In 1140 the Bishop of Lincoln founded a priory here, endowing it with various valuable possessions of the bishopric. As a result, the cathedral became Dorchester's abbey church. Thankfully, it was saved from demolition at the time of the Dissolution and purchased by a local resident for the modest sum of £140. He bequeathed the abbey church to the parish of Dorchester in his will.

The abbey remains at the heart of Dorchester and is a very special place in the history of Christianity in this country. Inside are many treasures that illustrate the abbey's long and distinguished history. The 12th-century lead font is decorated with figures of 11 apostles seated beneath a striking Romanesque arcade.

The nave is thought to have been built over the remains of the original cathedral and the east window is defined by a line of small sculptured figures depicting scenes from the life of Christ. Most of the glass in the top three rows dates from the early 14th century. The Jesse Window has 14th-century tracery, sculpture and stained glass bound together in one single theme. It depicts the story of how Christ was descended from King David's ancestor Jesse.

The Right Revd Robert Runcie, Archbishop of Canterbury 1980–91, described Dorchester Abbey as 'a building which keeps alive our sense of the sacred in a busy world', while John Betjeman said it was 'splendid in its proportions and details.'

Saving the Abbey

However, at the start of the 21st century Dorchester Abbey faces something of a crisis. A campaign has been launched to raise £5 million – the sum needed to make significant improvements to the abbey. The installation of a new heating system is required and work needs to be carried out to restore the shrine area as a place of prayer for peace and unity. Detailed plans have been drawn up and a lot of changes are expected, but no one doubts that the spirit and beauty of Dorchester Abbey will live on far into the future.

Walk 43

Walk 43 Directions

① From the parking area walk towards the centre of Dorchester, keeping the abbey church on the right. As you approach the **Fleur de Lys**, turn left into **Rotten Row** and walk along to **Mayflower Cottage** and **Pilgrims**. Take the path between the two properties and pass beside allotments. On reaching a row of cottages, veer left to follow a track. Swing right after 60yds (55m) at the sign for Day's Lock. Pass between fencing and out across a large field. Ahead is the outline of Wittenham Clumps. On reaching the low embankment of the **Dyke Hills**, turn right in front of the fence.

WHERE TO EAT AND DRINK ℹ

Dorchester's 16th-century **Fleur de Lys** offers morning coffee as well as drinks and home-cooked pub fare. Outside is a large beer garden. The **Kingfisher Inn** at Shillingford is open all day for snacks and meals. The **Shillingford Bridge Hotel** has a popular riverside restaurant and bar.

---

② Follow the path along the field edge, pass over a track and continue ahead. The path, enclosed by hedge and fencing, heads south towards the Thames riverbank. Go through a gate and follow the path, now unfenced, to a footbridge at **Day's Lock**. Cross the river to **Lock House Island** and head for **St Peter's Church** at Little Wittenham.

③ Turn left just beyond it, at the entrance to the manor. Keep right at the immediate fork, go through a galvanised gate and begin a steep climb to the viewpoint and beech trees on **Round Hill** at the top. Veer left as you approach a seat, pass a second seat and keep left at the next fork, heading for **Castle Hill**. Head

towards some gates at the foot of the hill, avoid a stile and go through a galvanised gate, up a flight of steps and into the trees. On reaching a T-junction, turn left.

WHILE YOU'RE THERE ℹ

Explore **Little Wittenham Nature Reserve**, established by the Northmoor Trust in 1982. Listen out for a fascinating variety of bird calls and songs from such species as robins, blackbirds and song thrushes and, in late autumn, the mistle thrush, fieldfare and redwing.

---

④ Emerge from the trees and pass the commemorative stone, keeping it on your right. Go down the grassy slope to a gate and pass through the trees to a field. Keep ahead along the perimeter, with woodland on the left. Pass a stile, continue along the field edge and round to the right in the corner. Swing left to join a nature trail and follow it through **Little Wittenham Wood**.

⑤ At a barrier and T-junction in the heart of the wood, turn left and follow the path back to **Little Wittenham**. Recross the Thames and then turn right to follow the river downstream. On reaching the confluence of the Thames and the Thame, swing left and head north towards Dorchester. As the Thame bends right, go straight on to a gate. Keep to the right of **Dyke Hills** to another gate and skirt the field to a track (**Wittenham Lane**). Pass the Catholic **Church of St Birinus** and return to the car park.

WHAT TO LOOK FOR ℹ

On Castle Hill is a beech tree known as the **Poem Tree**, with a poem carved by Joseph Tubb of Warborough Green, near Dorchester, in 1844–5. The nearby stone, commemorating the poem's 150th anniversary, was erected in 1994.

A Spur to Shillingford

Extend the walk by following a pretty stretch of the Thames.
See map and information panel for Walk 43

•DISTANCE•	7 miles (11.3km)
•MINIMUM TIME•	2hrs 45min
•ASCENT / GRADIENT•	Negligible
•LEVEL OF DIFFICULTY•	🚶 🚶 🚶

Walk 44 Directions (Walk 43 option)

Turn right at the T-junction in **Little Wittenham Wood** (Point Ⓐ) and cut through the wood. On breaking cover from the trees, continue along the edge of the field, maintaining the same direction. Keep to the track and, as you approach **North Farm**, turn right at the diversion sign, now heading south. The path was diverted in 1999. Take the first path on the left, cross a farm track and continue between fences and fields. Head down to rejoin the track, following it towards Shillingford. Avoid a turning on the right and at length the Thames edges into view, with Shillingford's classical bridge up ahead of you.

This reach of the river offers some of the finest scenery to be seen on the entire journey. The bank and surrounding countryside have always been very popular with tourists, cyclists and walkers. Built in 1827, balustraded and with three arches, Shillingford Bridge was originally built to carry the Wallingford to Thame turnpike over the river. The stretch of road here was turnpiked in 1764.

Walk through the car park of the **Shillingford Bridge Hotel** (Point Ⓑ) to reach the road. Turn left to cross the bridge and then swing left, following the Thames Path sign. When the track bears left, veer right by the entrance to **High Trees**. Go through a gate and follow the path between fencing.

Cross the entrance to **Shillingford Court** – it was here in 1809 that the Thames rose to such a height that it was above head level – and when the Thames Path turns left, continue along the enclosed path beside **Downgate House**. Keep ahead to the main road and turn left. Pass the **Kingfisher Inn** and follow the **A4074**.

On reaching a sign for Berinsfield and Dorchester, just before the road becomes a dual carriageway, cross over to a Thames Path sign and a kissing gate (Point Ⓒ). Go diagonally across the meadow to reach the riverside path, keeping the Thames on your left now. The point at which you reach the river represents the site of Keen Edge Ferry, one of the original ferry crossings on the Thames. Cross the **River Thame** at the bridge and then veer away from the national trail to follow the Thame riverbank, rejoining Walk 43.

Blewbury's Bleak Downland

Savour the stillness and solitude of Oxfordshire's racing country.

•DISTANCE•	7½ miles (12.1km)
•MINIMUM TIME•	3hrs
•ASCENT / GRADIENT•	160ft (49m) ▲▲▲
•LEVEL OF DIFFICULTY•	👥 👥 👥
•PATHS•	Downland paths, concrete farm roads and wide tracks
•LANDSCAPE•	Breezy open downland on Oxfordshire/Berkshire borders
•SUGGESTED MAP•	aqua3 OS Explorer 170 Abingdon, Wantage
•START / FINISH•	Grid reference: SU 532855
•DOG FRIENDLINESS•	On lead in Blewbury and under control by gallops
•PARKING•	Spaces in village, off A417
•PUBLIC TOILETS•	None on route

Walk 45 Directions

From the illustrated map of the village on the main A417, veer off to the right by a seat and follow the path to the springs. Walk along to an information board and turn right here, passing alongside one of Blewbury's picturesque thatched cob walls. Pass a thatched cottage called **Blue Haze**, turn left in front of the church and approach the village almshouses. Keep left here and take the little path. Veer left at the fork, cross a path and stream and then cut between the historic cob walls.

Join the road by the **Red Lion** and go straight on to the village war memorial, returning to the **A417**. Turn right and pass the **Blewbury Inn**. Opposite **Westbrook Street** turn left at the bridleway sign for the Ridgeway. Head south west on the path, pass a seat on the right and climb gently on to the downs. Cross a track and continue to **Churn Farm**. Turn right here, joining a concrete farm road

running between houses and outbuildings. Pass a cluster of brick and flint houses and turn left at the next junction.

Walk along to the next junction and ahead of you lies an old railway bridge. Turn left by a single-storey dwelling and follow the concrete track straight and true. Eventually it begins to curve left; at this point go straight on alongside a hedgerow. Follow a broad rutted track to the Ridgeway and continue ahead, following it up a gentle slope.

Britain's oldest road, the Ridgeway extends for 85 miles (137km) through the Buckinghamshire Chilterns to the Thames and then across Berkshire to touch Oxfordshire's southern boundary before reaching Wiltshire. In places the trail is as wide as a main road or a dual carriageway. When the original line became weathered or difficult to negotiate, travellers moved from one side to the other, gradually making the track wider. The character of the Ridgeway changes the further west you travel.

Initially, the trail cuts through gentle beechwood scenery, glorious in autumn, and across soft rolling hills where there are glimpses of distant horizons. Once across the Thames, the landscape assumes a totally different character. From the river onwards, the Ridgeway cuts across bleak, exposed downland, offering little in the way of shelter on a wet or windy day. Take a moment to savour the stillness of this magnificent downland country. On occasions I have stopped on this stretch and not heard a sound. It is hard to imagine being more remote or cut off from civilisation than here in this quiet, rural backwater. At times, it can be quite uncanny.

> ### WHERE TO EAT AND DRINK ⓘ
> The **Load of Mischief** and the **Blewbury Inn** both serve food and are situated on the main A417 in the centre of the village. The **Red Lion** in nearby Chapel Lane also has a popular menu. There are no pubs on the actual route, however.

Keep left at the next fork, draw level with a copse on the right, and then turn left at a crossroads. Cut between racing gallops, following the track with good views over to the right towards the Thames Valley and the familiar Wittenham Clumps (► Walk 43).

This part of Oxfordshire is synonymous with racehorse training. Racing as we know it today has its origins in the period of the Stuart kings. James I established stables at Newmarket and it was here that he kept racehorses and 'riders for the races' – the first royal jockeys. Towards the end of the 17th century, racehorses were beginning to appear all over the country, with many breeders introducing Arabian stock. Three of

> ### WHAT TO LOOK FOR ⓘ
> The old railway bridge at Churn gives a good view of the remains of **Churn Halt**, which closed many years ago. Before the First World War, soldiers came here by train to use the nearby rifle ranges, part of a tented army camp opened towards the end of the 19th century by Baron Wantage (► Walk 25), a pioneer of the territorial volunteers. The halt was on the old Didcot–Newbury–Southampton line.

these stallions were the sires from which all our thoroughbreds are descended. As the sport began to draw spectator interest, it split into two different categories – flat racing and racing over jumps.

Training stables for race horses were soon a permanent feature of life in the countryside, but they needed access to large tracts of open downland and grassland over which gallops could be laid for racing practice. As the flinty chalk soil made this landscape unsuitable for ploughing, the Berkshire Downs, embracing part of Oxfordshire, were considered ideal terrain for horses to compete with one another and for jockeys to sharpen and hone their skills.

Pass the buildings of **Woodway**; the track now graduates to a metalled lane. Follow the lane down to the **A417** and turn left. Pass the **Load of Mischief** pub and return to the map in **Blewbury** village centre.

> ### WHILE YOU'RE THERE ⓘ
> Take a good look at **Blewbury** and you'll be enchanted by its delightful thatched cottages and quaint cob walls, which date back to medieval times and were built to mark the boundaries of the many farms here. Kenneth Grahame, who wrote The Wind in the Willows, lived in the village between 1910 and 1924.

Jarn Mound – a Wild Garden and a Wonderful View

Discover how a local archaeologist moved the earth to protect a fine view of Oxford's famous skyline.

·DISTANCE·	5 miles (8km)
·MINIMUM TIME·	2hrs
·ASCENT / GRADIENT·	150ft (46m)
·LEVEL OF DIFFICULTY·	
·PATHS·	Field paths and tracks, roads (can be busy), 11 stiles
·LANDSCAPE·	Hilly, well-wooded country south west of Oxford
·SUGGESTED MAP·	aqua3 OS Explorer 180 Oxford
·START / FINISH·	Grid reference: SP 496005
·DOG FRIENDLINESS·	On lead at Jarn Mound and on farmland
·PARKING·	Limited spaces in Sunningwell
·PUBLIC TOILETS·	None on route

BACKGROUND TO THE WALK

When the archaeologist Sir Arthur Evans (1851–1941) built Jarn Mound, it was with the intention of providing a panoramic view across Oxfordshire towards the neighbouring counties of Warwickshire and Berkshire. However, if Evans were to climb the steps to this noted viewpoint today, he would be dismayed to discover trees and modern housing development had radically changed the character of the landscape.

It was in 1928 that the Oxford Preservation Trust purchased 64 acres (26ha) of land here on Boars Hill in order to preserve the view of Oxford and her dreaming spires (► Walk 8). A local resident and a leading figure in the world of archaeology, renowned for his discoveries at Knossos in Crete, Evans suggested to the Trust that it go one better in an effort to preserve the view from Matthew Arnold's signal-elm, which looked towards the Berkshire Downs, the Vale of White Horse, the River Thames and Oxford.

A Mound with a View

With the support of the Trust, Evans pledged to create an artificial mound to provide a wider view of the area. For as long as anyone could remember, the site had been known locally as Jarn. This was possibly a corruption of the French word for garden.

Despite huge problems, including constant soil slippage, work on the mound was eventually finished. It took nearly three years and was completed in November 1931. The task was perfect for Evans, the epitomal archaeologist, and he revelled in the challenge of erecting a 50ft (15m) high mound. On the summit was placed the dial plate indicating the distances between the mound and significant places of interest in the area. A bowl of freshly minted coins was placed inside.

But Evans didn't stop there. He was keen to enclose the mound so that it blended with its surroundings, and to achieve this his next project was to establish a wild garden of British plants, having first gained the approval of the Oxford Preservation Trust. He imported appropriate soils to allow a variety of native flora to thrive here. The pit created by the building of the mound was transformed into rock and bog gardens and a pond, which was partly re-excavated in 1992.

Most people would applaud Evans's efforts to raise Jarn Mound and create this garden, and it seems ironic that, after everything he did to provide a magnificent viewpoint for people to enjoy, the vistas he intended to preserve have now become so restricted. In fact, other parts of this hilly district, including a stretch of road on this walk, offer much clearer views of Oxford's glorious skyline.

Walk 46 Directions

① Walk along the village street towards Abingdon. Pass a pond on the right and the church on the left and, as the road bends left, turn right into **Dark Lane**. Keep the cricket ground on your right and soon the lane becomes a concrete track. When it curves right, keep

left, following a rough track between hedgerows and then across open fields. Didcot Power Station can be seen from here.

② Take a track running to the right towards farm outbuildings and cut between them. Continue on the track between trees to the road and turn right. Follow the verge to a sign for Old Boars Hill and take the path. Cross the open field, pass through a boundary hedge and keep ahead towards a white house. Look for a stile in the field corner beside it and cross the lane to a stile and gate.

③ Follow the metalled lane to **The Linnings,** a riding school. Keep to the right of the buildings, crossing three stiles. Go diagonally across the paddock, passing under power lines, to reach the boundary hedge. Cross two stiles, avoiding stiles in the left and right boundary of the field, and follow the path beside a high wire fence enclosing a reservoir. Keep ahead at the fence corner to a galvanised gate and stile on the right and follow an enclosed path beside a paddock towards the houses of Wootton. Cross a stile and turn right, passing the entrance to **Stones Farm.**

WHERE TO EAT AND DRINK ⓘ

The **Flowing Well** at Sunningwell has been a pub since about 1950. It was originally the local rectory. Recently refurbished and given a new image, the pub serves food daily, as well as a traditional roast on Sunday.

---

④ On reaching the entrance to **Wootton End** on the left, keep right here, following a track. Go through a galvanised gate and keep to the right of a pond. Head up the slope to a stile and cross **Matthew Arnold's Field** to a stile leading out

to the lane. Turn left and walk along to the junction with **Jarn Way.** Climb to **Jarn Mound,** then descend the steps and turn left by the seat, keeping the memorial stone on the left. Keep parallel with the road, veer left at the fork and follow the path to the road. Turn right, pass a house called **Holly Dene** and go down to the junction.

WHILE YOU'RE THERE ⓘ

Sunningwell church, at the start of the walk, is famous in Oxfordshire for its curious, multi-sided porch built by John Jewel who was rector here and later became Bishop of Salisbury. Roger Bacon, the famous 13th-century scientist, used the tower to make astronomical observations.

---

⑤ Go straight on into **Berkeley Road,** passing the former Open University building on the right-hand side. There is a clear view of the Sheldonian Theatre and many of Oxford's other historic landmarks from this stretch of the road. Walk along to the T-junction and turn right. Head for **Lincombe Lane** and a sign for Sunningwell. Follow the road round to the right, pass a footpath and continue all the way to a white gate and a kissing gate. Follow the field path towards **Sunningwell church.** Go through a gate at the bottom of the field, emerge at the road opposite the church, and return to the start of the walk.

WHAT TO LOOK FOR ⓘ

As you undertake this walk, you'll find **information boards** telling you about the Oxford Preservation Trust, which was founded in 1927 and is thought to be the oldest amenity society in the country. Its aim is to protect and improve historic Oxford and preserve its unique green setting. The Trust works to protect the city's architectural heritage, and, among many successful projects, has restored Magdalen Bridge, one of Oxford's finest landmarks. Matthew Arnold's Field is owned by the Oxford Preservation Trust. Arnold described this part of Oxfordshire in *The Scholar Gypsy and Thyrsis* and the Trust considered this wonderful heritage site too valuable to be lost to development.

Greys Court – a House and a Home

Visit a National Trust property in a delightfully unspoiled setting on this pretty walk in the Chilterns.

•DISTANCE•	4 miles (6.4km)
•MINIMUM TIME•	1hr 45min
•ASCENT / GRADIENT•	150ft (45m)
•LEVEL OF DIFFICULTY•	
•PATHS•	Field and parkland paths, drives and tracks, stretches of road (can be busy), 12 stiles
•LANDSCAPE•	Chiltern hills and farmland, Greys Court parkland
•SUGGESTED MAP•	aqua3 OS Explorer 171 Chiltern Hills West
•START / FINISH•	Grid reference: SU 726823
•DOG FRIENDLINESS•	Several dog stiles. Under control by golf course and in vicinity of Greys Court
•PARKING•	Spaces by church at Rotherfield Greys
•PUBLIC TOILETS•	Greys Court, for visitors; otherwise none on route

BACKGROUND TO THE WALK

There is a charming intimacy about Greys Court, a delightfully homely air that is not always evident in properties that have been immaculately restored and preserved by the National Trust. During my visit there I found the usual quota of attractions, but there were also signs of a familiar domestic routine. A television set stood in one of the ground floor rooms and in the kitchen I spotted a member of staff making tea for the lady of the house. Even when it opens its doors to the public, Greys Court retains a strong 'lived-in' feel – this is not just a house, but a home.

Romantic Ruins

The flint walls and ivy-clad towers are all that remain of a sizeable 14th-century crenellated mansion belonging to the Lords Grey of Rotherfield. Within them Sir William Knollys, Earl of Banbury, built a manor house in 1605. His father, Francis Knollys, had been treasurer to Elizabeth I. Greys Court passed to Sir William Stapleton in the 1720s. His descendants remained here until 1935.

During the time the house was occupied by the Stapletons, the estate comprised a staggering 8,000 acres (3,240ha) of woodland, parkland and farmland. Today, it covers a more modest 300 acres (121.5ha), with the delightful 16th-century house, standing beside the ruins of the old fortified manor, at its heart.

One of Greys Court's most popular attractions is its picturesque garden. When Sir Felix and Lady Brunner moved here in 1937, they found this area of the estate to be sadly neglected. War was declared soon after their arrival, so very little work was undertaken until the late 1940s. However, when it came to planning improvements to the garden, the Brunners found the old walls of the fortified manor gave them a distinct advantage over many other country houses.

The gardener's statue in the Kitchen Garden commemorates Charles Taylor, who was Head Gardener at Greys Court between 1937 and 1955. It was he who helped Lady Brunner rescue the garden and give it new life. The iron pergola linking the Kitchen Garden and the Wisteria Garden includes the initials of Sir Felix and Lady Brunner, and was commissioned to mark their golden wedding in 1977. The wisteria has the effect of binding the various gardens and is best appreciated in early May.

The White Garden was inspired by the renowned gardens of Sissinghurst in Kent, the work of Sir Harold Nicolson and his wife, the writer Victoria (Vita) Sackville-West. This was the first garden at Greys Court to be restored and it was completed in the mid-1950s. The old glasshouse was demolished and stone slabs from the kitchen were used to pave the new summer house and terrace. The pond was created to mark a family engagement.

Walk 47 Directions

① With the church lychgate on your left-hand side, walk towards the **Maltsters Arms** pub and turn

immediately left before **William's Cottage** to join a gravel drive. Follow the footpath alongside the churchyard and make for the stile ahead. Head obliquely right, across the field to another stile, pass

Walk 47

through the gap in the hedgerow
and then veer half-right in the next
field. Make for a stile, cross over
and join a path.

② Turn right and pass between
trees, high hedges and margins of
bracken. The path graduates to
become a track and passes alongside
the fairways of a golf course before
crossing a drive to a gate. Continue
ahead to reach the road and turn
right. Pass a turning for Shepherd's
Green on the left and follow the
road along to the grassy expanse
of **Greys Green**. Veer left on to the
green and aim to the right of the
pavilion. Join a footpath, cross a
stile and descend very steeply to the
next stile. Pass under power lines in
the pasture and keep the fence on
the left. Make for a stile, cross a lane
to a footpath and after a few steps
you reach a stile. Continue ahead
towards **Greys Court**.

③ Walk along to the admission
kiosk and swing left here, following
the footpath to the next boundary.
Continue on the path to a pond and
along a section of boardwalk. Pass

alongside a fence and woodland,
avoiding a gate and some steps to
reach a stile on the left just beyond
them by a corrugated barn. Cross
over the stile and keep to the right-
hand side, with the fence and field
on the right. Turn right at a drive
and make for the road ahead. Turn
right at this junction and continue,
passing **Broadplat**.

④ Keep left at the next junction
and continue along the road to
reach a track on the right,
signposted to Rotherfield Greys.
Continue ahead when the track
bends to the left, and follow a rough
track ahead. Pass a footpath sign
and look for a stile on the left.
Follow the path down the hillside,
keeping a belt of woodland on the
right. Beyond it, continue on the
grassy path with a fence on the
right. Turn right, across a stile in
the field corner and follow the path
alongside fencing. After about 60yds
(55m), look for a stile on the left.
Cross it and maintain the same
direction. Make for a stile ahead,
then swing left and follow the path
up the slope and back to the road
opposite the church at **Rotherfield
Greys** where you started the walk.

Stoke Row and a Maharajah's Gift

Discover the link between India and a quiet English village on this pleasant walk in the Chilterns.

•DISTANCE•	5 miles (8km)
•MINIMUM TIME•	2hrs
•ASCENT / GRADIENT•	164ft (50m)
•LEVEL OF DIFFICULTY•	
•PATHS•	Field and woodland paths and tracks, road (busy), 8 stiles
•LANDSCAPE•	Chiltern woodland and farmland
•SUGGESTED MAP•	aqua3 OS Explorer 171 Chiltern Hills West
•START / FINISH•	Grid reference: SU 678840
•DOG FRIENDLINESS•	On lead in Stoke Row and Cherry Orchard; under control where indicated. On lead where indicated on Walk 49
•PARKING•	Roadside parking in Stoke Row; two spaces in village hall car park when hall not in use
•PUBLIC TOILETS•	None on route

BACKGROUND TO THE WALK

It is unusual, to say the least, and not what you would expect to find in an English village. Enclosed by an exotic cupola, the Maharajah's Well might be a familiar landmark in Stoke Row but first-time visitors gaze curiously at this spectacle, unsure at first if they can believe what they are seeing.

The well was given to the village by the Maharajah of Benares in 1863 as a gift. But where, you might ask, is the connection with Stoke Row? It was on a Benares hillside, around the middle of the 19th century, that the Indian ruler met Edward Anderdon Reade, who was soon to become Lieutenant-Governor of the North West Provinces of India. The Maharajah indicated his plans to overcome the acute water shortage in the area and Anderdon Reade responded by pointing out that it was a familiar problem at home in the Chilterns where his father ran an estate.

A Precious Resource

In villages like Stoke Row, he told the Maharajah, local people relied on rainwater for their cooking, and so precious was it that it was often passed from one cooking pot to the next. Neighbours shared what water they could collect and children were often punished for drinking it to quench their thirst. Pond water was used for washing and when that ran out, wash day was postponed, sometimes indefinitely.

During the Indian Mutiny, Edward Anderdon Reade offered help and support to the Maharajah of Benares, who had not forgotten Stoke Row and the ongoing problem of its water supply. To express his gratitude for the Lieutenant-Governor's solidarity at a difficult time, and as a token of friendship, the Maharajah presented the village with a charitable gift.

The local Commissioners chose a suitable site in Stoke Row and the Maharajah duly approved it, recommending that construction work should commence on the wedding day of the Prince of Wales, later Edward VII. The date was 10 March 1863. Building began with the sinking of a 4ft (1.2m) wide well to a depth of 368ft (112m), more than twice the height of Nelson's Column. All the work was done by hand.

The well was officially opened 14 months later on 24 May 1864 – Queen Victoria's birthday. A condition of the gift was 'that the public should have the privilege of taking water free of charge in all time to come.' A small cottage was built beside the well, housing a warden who would manage it.

The beneficent Maharajah did not forget the village and in later years donated other gifts. For example, to mark the wedding of Princess Louise he created a new footpath leading to the well and also gave £200 so that the villagers could host thanksgiving celebrations. In 1906 mains water was piped to Stoke Row and in 1927 a second pipeline brought water from Nettlebed. Even so, some residents continued to use the well and it was still in use in 1939.

Walk **48**

Walk 48 Directions

① From the car park turn right and walk past the village stores. Turn left into **Cox's Lane** and follow it as it curves to the left. Soon it dwindles to a track. Continue to a waymark, avoid the footpath on the right and keep ahead on the right of way. The track narrows to a path now, running between trees and hedgerows. Pass a stile and footpath and eventually you reach the outbuildings of **Hundridge Farm**. Join a track running through the woodland and make for the road.

> ### WHILE YOU'RE THERE
> If you've time, visit **Wellplace Zoo** at nearby Ipsden. Opened in 1968, the zoo is a very popular family attraction in the area. It has a large and varied collection of birds and animals from all parts of the world including lemurs, flamingos, penguins, parrots and owls. There is also a small museum devoted to village life, and an education centre.

② Turn right along the road for several paces, then swing right at the footpath sign into the wood. Follow the path between trees and cross a drive. Make for a stile ahead and then go diagonally right in the field, using the waymark posts to guide you. Look for a stile in the

> ### WHAT TO LOOK FOR
> Together with the adjoining well, the **Cherry Orchard** was given to the village by the Maharajah of Benares. One hundred and one cherry trees were originally planted to provide an income to help fund the upkeep of the well, though today the orchard is a village open space, its upkeep dependent on donations and support from the parish council. A number of features within the orchard were given Indian names.

corner and cross a lane to a further stile on the opposite side. Head diagonally right in the field and look for a stile by a hard tennis court. Pass alongside a beech hedge to a drive and turn left. As the drive sweeps left to a house, go forward over a cattle grid to a field. Continue with the boundary on your left and on reaching the corner, go straight on along a track.

> ### WHERE TO EAT AND DRINK
> The **Crooked Billet** at Stoke Row is a popular rustic country pub with the emphasis very much on food. Once one of Dick Turpin's hideouts, it retains lots of old-world charm and atmosphere. The actress Kate Winslet held her wedding reception here. The quality, award-winning menu is made up of local produce and organic ingredients.

③ Turn right at **English Farm** and follow the narrow track known as **English Lane**. Pass a footpath and stile on the right-hand side and follow the track along the edge of woodland. Continue to a junction and keep ahead through the trees. Pass a timber-framed cottage on the left-hand side and a house on the right called **Forrigan**. Keep ahead for about 100yds (91m) and swing right at a sign for Stoke Row.

④ Cross a stile and cut through the wood to a second stile. Emerge from the woodland at a gate and cross a pasture to a further patch of woodland. Negotiate the next stile within sight of the **Crooked Billet** (► Where to Eat and Drink) and go up a gentle slope towards the pub. Turn right at the road, pass a footpath on the right, followed by **Rose Cottage**, and head for the crossroads in the centre of **Stoke Row**. Turn right and return to the start of the walk.

A Loop to Nuffield

Extend the walk to a scattered hilltop village.
See map and information panel for Walk 48

•DISTANCE•	3½ miles (5.7km)
•MINIMUM TIME•	1hr 30min
•ASCENT / GRADIENT•	150ft (46m) ▲▲▲
•LEVEL OF DIFFICULTY•	👫 👫 👫

Walk 49 Directions
(Walk 48 option)

Turn left at **English Farm** and follow the lane to the road junction (Point Ⓐ). Turn left for several paces and cross over to a footpath, following it to the left of a line of trees. Cross the field, passing under power lines, and at the far hedge go through the gap and turn right. Pass through some trees to reach the **Ridgeway**, which follows an ancient earthwork, Grim's Ditch, to the west. Go straight on towards **Nuffield**.

Climb gently through a belt of woodland and emerge by a galvanised gate. Follow the field edge ahead to the road and turn right (Point Ⓑ). Pass the 900-year-old church with its helpful sign for the benefit of Ridgeway walkers: 'Water tap on the church wall at the base of the tower. The church is normally open and you are welcome to use it for shelter in wet weather.'

The church is 700ft (213m) above sea level and the highest point in the southern Chilterns. Two thousand years ago, this would have been a site of Druidic worship involving human sacrifice. The Roman invasion brought law and order, and

this hilltop almost certainly became the setting for a Roman villa. Some of the tiles have been incorporated into the church tower.

The churchyard contains the grave of the renowned car manufacturer and benefactor William Morris, (1877–1963) (➤ Walk 9), who fell in love with this lofty village and took its name as Viscount Nuffield. He lived at nearby Nuffield Place.

Continue along the road through the village, parting company with the Ridgeway now. Pass the former village school, now a private house, and make for the junction with **Timbers Lane**. Cross over and pass to the left of a house called **Martyns Close**. Follow the path to a gravelled drive by some houses and pass **Elderberry Cottage** on the right.

Keep ahead on an enclosed bridleway, between trees and bushes. On reaching a track at length, turn right and shortly you come to a sign for Howberrywood farm. Cross the stile here and go diagonally right across the field, aiming for some trees just to the left of **English Farm**. Look for a gate leading out to a track, keep right and follow it as it curves left. Pass left of the farm outbuildings to reach a junction of tracks and then rejoin Walk 48.

Walk 50

Mapledurham – Screen Star

Visit a remote village used as a film and television location on this pretty walk.

•DISTANCE•	3 miles (4.8km)
•MINIMUM TIME•	1hr 15min
•ASCENT / GRADIENT•	164ft (50m)
•LEVEL OF DIFFICULTY•	
•PATHS•	Mainly farm tracks and field paths, 1 stile
•LANDSCAPE•	Parkland and farmland on northern bank of Thames
•SUGGESTED MAP•	aqua3 OS Explorer 159 Reading
•START / FINISH•	Grid reference: SU 670767
•DOG FRIENDLINESS•	On lead in Mapledurham, under control elsewhere
•PARKING•	Permission kindly given for walkers to use small car park adjacent to church
•PUBLIC TOILETS•	Mapledurham House, for visitors; otherwise none on route

Walk 50 Directions

Mapledurham and its timeless Thames setting in the south east corner of Oxfordshire create an idyllic picture. The village is one of only a few settlements in the area that have not been blighted by urban development. The lack of a road bridge providing a direct link with nearby Reading has, in effect, ruled out the possibility of expansion, and Mapledurham remains a sleepy, rather isolated village approached down narrow winding lanes running deep into the heart of the countryside. Not surprisingly, life in this part of the world tends to be on the quiet and uneventful side.

However, it was a very different story back in 1976. If you could somehow transform yourself back in time to the very hot summer of that year you would have found Mapledurham a hive of activity. The village might have been hard to recognise too – and, even more

puzzling, its name had changed to Studley Constable. An old-fashioned dairy shop displayed gleaming milk churns in the window; stirrup pumps and baby Austins added to the nostalgic picture of rural England; and, perhaps most bizzare of all, there were signposts to the east-coast port of King's Lynn.

Almost everywhere you went, there was a genuine feeling that the village had stood still since the Second World War. But why? What did it all mean? Still mystified? The clue is in the title of this walk. Mapledurham was doubling as a film set for the celluloid version of *The Eagle Has Landed*, a classic adventure yarn by thriller writer Jack Higgins. If you have read the book or seen the film, then you'll know the plot concerns an attempt

> **WHERE TO EAT AND DRINK** ⓘ
> There are no inns in Mapledurham but at nearby Chazey Heath the **Pack Saddle** pub offers food every day. **Mapledurham House** has a tea room.

Walk 50

to kidnap Winston Churchill (► Walks 21 and 22) while he is spending the weekend at a country house in Norfolk in 1943.

Much of the film, which stars Michael Caine and Donald Sutherland, was shot at Mapledurham, and the village Church of St Margaret, where the villagers are held captive, features prominently. However, if you expect to get a drink at the delightfully named Spyglass and Kettle, you'll be disappointed. The pub was a fake – a clever illusion created by film designers and artists.

WHILE YOU'RE THERE ⓘ

Visit **Mapledurham House**, completed in the late 16th century by Sir Richard Blount for his Catholic family. Built of red brick with stone dressings, Mapledurham is one of the largest and most famous Elizabethan houses in Oxfordshire. The house contains a priest hole and there is also an 10th-century private chapel, visible from the adjacent churchyard.

Some crucial sequences of the film were shot by the 15th-century corn mill, where Nazi infiltrators, posing as Polish soldiers, inadvertently blow their cover. The mill, distinguished by an undershot wooden waterwheel, has two pairs of millstones which are used to produce wholemeal flour.

Easy access to London and the success of *The Eagle Has Landed* have resulted in Mapledurham being regularly chosen as a location for film and television productions. They include *Class Act* starring Joanna Lumley, and *Inspector Morse* with the late John Thaw as the world-famous Oxford sleuth. The gently lapping Thames, imposing Mapledurham House and neat rows

of handsome houses in the main street create just the right images for the large and small screen – the quintessential English village.

From the small car park by the church, turn right and walk along the village street to a bridleway on the right, signposted to Caversham. Pass the lodge on the corner and follow the concrete track through the parkland. This stretch of the walk offers lovely views over wooded countryside and fields, with the Thames away to the right. Pass the isolated buildings of **Park Farm** and look back for a good view of Mapledurham House.

Follow the track to the next lodge and turn left. Keep left at the next junction, with the grain store on the right, and head up the track into the trees. Break cover and continue to the next junction. Keep left here, and again there are good views over Berkshire and Oxfordshire. Follow the track round several bends and make for the next farm.

Turn left at the road and follow it until you reach a path on the left where the lane curves right. Follow the path and pass through a galvanised gate. Walk ahead to the next gate and cross the field, keeping the brick and timber-framed **Step Cottage** to your right. Avoid the stile leading out to the road and continue crossing the field, eventually curving to the left at the point where you see the road ahead.

The walk crosses a slope and then runs parallel with the lane leading to Mapledurham. Look for 'passing place' signs on the road and make for a stile. Descend the bank to the lane and turn left for **Mapledurham House** and the village centre.

Walking in Safety

All these walks are suitable for any reasonably fit person, but less experienced walkers should try the easier walks first. Route finding is usually straightforward, but you will find that an Ordnance Survey map is a useful addition to the route maps and descriptions.

Risks

Although each walk here has been researched with a view to minimising the risks to the walkers who follow its route, no walk in the countryside can be considered to be completely free from risk. Walking in the outdoors will always require a degree of common sense and judgement to ensure that it is as safe as possible.

- Be particularly careful on cliff paths and in upland terrain, where the consequences of a slip can be very serious.

- Remember to check tidal conditions before walking on the seashore.

- Some sections of route are by, or cross, busy roads. Take care and remember traffic is a danger even on minor country lanes.

- Be careful around farmyard machinery and livestock, especially if you have children with you.

- Be aware of the consequences of changes in the weather and check the forecast before you set out. Carry spare clothing and a torch if you are walking in the winter months. Remember the weather can change very quickly at any time of the year, and in moorland and heathland areas, mist and fog can make route finding much harder. Don't set out in these conditions unless you are confident of your navigation skills in poor visibility. In summer remember to take account of the heat and sun; wear a hat and carry spare water.

- On walks away from centres of population you should carry a whistle and survival bag. If you do have an accident requiring the emergency services, make a note of your position as accurately as possible and dial 999.

Acknowledgements

My grateful thanks to the staff of Broughton Castle, Rousham House, Hook Norton Brewery, New College, Oxford, the Rollright Stones, Chastleton House, Blenheim Palace, Vale and Downland Museum, Ardington Estate, Cogges Manor Farm Museum, Didcot Railway Centre, Warburg Nature Reserve Visitor Centre, Stonor Park, Cholsey and Wallingford railway, Kelmscott Manor, Dorchester Abbey, Oxford Preservation Trust, Greys Court, Mapledurham House and the various libraries, public houses and tourist information centres.

AQUA3 AA Publishing and Outcrop Publishing Services would like to thank Chartech for supplying aqua3 maps for this book.
For more information visit their website: www.aqua3.com.

Series management: Outcrop Publishing Services Limited, Cumbria
Series editor: Chris Bagshaw **Copy editor:** Jenni Davis
Front cover: AA Photo Library/S Day **Back cover:** AA Photo Library/J Martin